Mereo Books

1A The Wool Market Dyer Street Cirencester Gloucestershire GL7 2PR
An imprint of Memoirs Publishing www.mereobooks.com

Yesterday's Countryside, Tomorrow's Choices: 978-1-86151-887-3

First published in Great Britain in 2018
by Mereo Books, an imprint of Memoirs Publishing

Copyright ©2018

The address for Memoirs Publishing Group Limited can be found at www.memoirspublishing.com

The Memoirs Publishing Group Ltd Reg. No. 7834348

Typeset in 12/18pt Bembo
by Wiltshire Associates Publisher Services Ltd. Printed and bound
in Great Britain by Biddles Books

PROLOGUE

This book has two distinct sections. Firstly it gives a personal account of growing up and working in the countryside since the mid-sixties and describes how much our English countryside has changed over the last 50 years. This is based on practical experiences recorded in diaries and learning from observation while growing up and working professionally in countryside management in Gloucestershire, Bedfordshire, Surrey, Cheshire and the south-west of England, including iconic and protected landscapes.

In Part 2 of the book, the author uses his acquired knowledge of nature and our attempts to conserve the countryside over 50 years to make very timely suggestions on the choices to be made on how our lost countryside can be restored once again to a rich and thriving place for nature. The recent publication of the 25-year Environment Plan and announcement by Michael Gove, Secretary of State for the Environment, Food and Rural Affairs, on future farming subsidies placing a greater emphasis on environmental enhancements is welcome. This book includes recommendations on best practices that can and should be

Paul B Rutter

YESTERDAY'S COUNTRYSIDE
COUNTRYSIDE
Tomorrow's Choices

A COMPREHENSIVE INSIGHT INTO THE PROBLEMS
AND SOLUTIONS OF TODAY'S ENVIRONMENT

PAUL B RUTTER

YESTERDAY'S COUNTRYSIDE
Tomorrow's Choices

A COMPREHENSIVE INSIGHT INTO THE PROBLEMS
AND SOLUTIONS OF TODAY'S ENVIRONMENT

MEMOIRS

Cirencester

adopted to restore the biodiversity that has been lost or damaged so badly over the last 50 years at least.

The broad ranging benefits we all enjoy by having a healthy environment and functioning countryside are also explained, illustrating how it affects all of all our lives as well as the wildlife, while also highlighting the many environmental threats that we face.

An alternative structure to the current Department of Environment is also included to suggest ways of implementing much of what is highlighted in the book.

CONTENTS

INTRODUCTION

I have worked professionally in the great outdoors, with and for nature, for over 45 years. It has kept me very busy, so just over a year ago I finally sat down to begin to record this account of what has been an eventful and very satisfying life so far. Over much of this time I have had an enjoyable and rewarding life and successfully pursued my passion to protect, conserve and manage the natural world as my chosen career. Although far from being a financially rewarding career, it has nevertheless given me many unique and inspiring experiences with wild animals and the natural world.

This book recounts my direct experience of many those close encounters that I have had with wild nature from a very early age which I recorded in diaries for over 40 years, which have helped me to reflect on what I have observed and learnt over that time, while also recording many of my achievements.

Using my unique experience and acquired knowledge I also look ahead to suggest solutions to the many environmental issues that we face today. I offer a pragmatic and common sense approach to the way we can protect, manage and enhance a somewhat depleted and impoverished ecosystem in an increasingly threatened and changing landscape.

I am writing at a time of potential significant change in our countryside so I hope the reader finds it entertaining, topical and informative.

CHAPTER 1

WHERE IT ALL BEGAN

I have always been content to be different from other people, more interested in learning from direct experience rather than by formal education, by listening and learning from the people who live and work in the countryside and by my own observations, then acting on my gut instincts. Being determined, as well and having a curious mind, are qualities that I have used to achieve my ambition and to take on the many personal challenges of pursuing this unorthodox career.

Perhaps my curiosity and concern for the natural world were passed on from my grandfather Frederick Brueton. Although I never knew him I may have inherited a gene from him that influenced my fascination and concern about our beautiful natural world. My grandfather was chief planner for the city of Bristol in the 1930s. He was someone who was very concerned about the loss of countryside and green space being lost and replaced by housing and development.

Working with the distinguished town planner Patrick Abercrombie, they published a book in 1929 called *The Regional Planning Scheme for Bristol and Bath*, and in it they included the importance of green open spaces being protected from development around the cities of Bristol and Bath. These included the provision of communal open spaces, parks for recreation, while also protecting what they termed in the book as *remarkable* landscapes. Frederick Brueton's legacy is the inclusion of trees and hedges as part of any new housing scheme around Bristol in the 1930s. Sea Mills is just one good example of what was achieved. Eighty years later much of what the book recommended is even more relevant to us today.

Quote from his book 1929:

The author would like to draw the attention of the (Joint Planning) Committee to the need for immediate action: at this moment buildings are being erected in the Region that are unworthy of their situation and without due regard to their position, advertisements erected in the line of vision of famous views, petrol stations present disorderly fronts to main roads and destroy the charm of village streets. These are obvious defects but equally important deviations from just forms of development are going on where there is no planning scheme in operation. Town planning should be applied to the whole region if an economic and orderly future is to be secured to this singularly beautiful country and these attractive towns and villages

Many years after the book was written, I was born and I remember as I grew up being greatly concerned about the loss of our flora and fauna by what I was seeing happening around me in my own local environment on edge of Bristol.

On my very own doorstep around my home I was becoming increasingly aware of the impact that man was having on the local environment. Whenever I looked out from my bedroom window I could see white and yellow smoke and steam billowing from tall, slender chimneys, emitting goodness knows what from nearby industrial complexes at Severnside. These industries were just a few miles down the road, constantly emitting a hum and glowing brightly all day and night. Even the sparrows and trees around them were blackened by the smutty, polluted air!

I grew up in a village called Hallen near Bristol with my parents, brother and sister. My mother was owner of a pony and trap. Her passion was for horses and before I could even walk she would take us out for rides in the trap. We went along the quiet lanes around our home accompanied by Tuppence, a dark bay pony. This was my early introduction to nature and my local environment.

The birds would stay close by as we clip clopped along the stony tracks and tarmacked lanes, we could see them so clearly, perched in tree branches and in the tall hedgerows. Sitting in the trap the wild animals and birds held no fear of us as we were pulled along by a horse while the bipedal human, from the dawn of time, hunted animals for food, so they have become programmed to flee whenever humans were smelt, heard or seen.

My village was surrounded by traditional farmed landscape in the Severn Valley. This was a typical piece of countryside surrounded by permanent pastures and hay meadows enclosed by thick hedges. A network of deep ditches, locally called rhines, was another feature and the banks were dotted with old pollarded ash trees and crack willows. Nearby on a hill overlooking the village was an ancient oak, ash and hazel woodland with elm and an occasional Scots pine completed this tranquil scene that I called my home.

The narrow lanes had tall overarching elm trees which sadly began dying from Dutch Elm Disease (DED) in 1968. We were near to Avonmouth docks, thought to be one of the sites where the disease was imported into the country some years earlier from America.

Before they all died from DED, we spent many hours climbing the elm trees during a time of innocent freedom when we were able to explore the countryside and use our common sense to learn about risk, as we call it today, which was all just part of growing up really.

Despite the ever-present risk of tree climbing being practiced by all my friends, on only one occasion did anyone actually fall out of a tree, when one day a young girl unfortunately broke her leg. We all took note and remembered this event. It was, however, never thought to be a reason to ban us from tree climbing, thankfully.

My close encounters with birds, trees and nature during our pony and trap rides had sparked an interest that became a lifelong passion. The instinctive fear that wildlife had towards humans was something I later tried to challenge on my walks by stalking wildlife and to get as near as possible to see their beautiful features and watch their behaviour close up. I also tried to record birdsong on a portable tape recorder, with limited success, and then began to draw and take photographs of wildlife.

The best way of learning about the natural world is to observe it first hand in the field. I spent time sitting quietly looking closely at what I saw around me, exploring a hollow tree or a bush to find bird nests and many other things that would otherwise be passed by and which other people would be quite oblivious to.

At the age of eight I had two friends Lyn and Alan who had seen a lot of the world having moved from Australia to England, and through their early global experiences introduced me to the World Wildlife Fund, now the Worldwide Fund for Nature. Their work highlighted the plight of elephants, rhinos and tigers that were being slaughtered, pandas that were close to extinction, the elephants and rhinos that were being killed for their ivory and horn.

It is so frustrating that, 50 years later, little seems to have changed today because their decline by mindless butchery continues... although I understand that tiger numbers are recovering at the time of writing this book and at last giant pandas are breeding.

Nearer to home and despite the expansion of industrial complexes steadily expanding onto more green fields, the few small farms that still remained continued their daily routine of milking the cows each day and making hay in summer. I often helped on these farms with haymaking, cutting thistles and bagging up potatoes. (I cut two fields of thistles once for a 10 shilling note, 50p in today's currency.) Herding the cows into the milk parlour each evening, they were milked by hand while I sat on a three legged stool, we then rolled the churns of milk up to the farm gate for collection by the nearby dairy. I remember a new-fangled milking machine later being brought in to do the work almost automatically, once the teats had been fitted with the suckers to draw off the milk.

Getting the hay stacked on trailers and taken to barns was always a sociable and fun time, and we were able to enjoy the flower-rich meadows that this farming had maintained for centuries. We rode horses, played games in the fields, did pond dipping in the rhines and scattered ponds finding sticklebacks, newts, diving beetles and so much more.

Being so passionate about horses, for our own up-bringing, my mother followed best principles of horse husbandry and ensured we children always had a clean bed, fresh food and regular exercise. It seemed to work!

We were taught to ride almost before we could walk and I well remember at the age of four falling off the back end of big grey mare while in an orchard with low hanging trees. Nobody seemed very concerned assuming that we had soft bones and that young people bounced at that age!!

As we grew older we were given regular tasks at home to look after what at times was over 20 animals and birds. This included cleaning out the animals, feeding the rabbits, guinea pigs, hamster, chickens and ducks and various gardening tasks in our quite large garden. Walking the dog was also one of the daily routines and I loved to get outside to explore the countryside, and pursue my hobby of enjoying nature and looking for the wildlife.

While out walking I spent many hours patiently waiting and watching, sitting up in trees or under hedgerows and was often rewarded by a view of a kestrel hovering nearby or by a fox stealthily patrolling the field margins.

From December 1968 I began recording my observations in a notebook, noting down all that I saw on my walks. I suppose I could be described as an early twitcher. Reading it today is a sobering reminder of the vibrant landscape in which I lived and records all the species I regularly saw. This was a countryside considered then to be nothing very special at the time. Today, just 45 years later that same countryside has been largely lost forever, buried under roads, waste landfill, warehouses and industrial units. This is just one small part of countryside which together with so many thousands of acres have also been lost across the British Isles in a very short time.

It is because of this loss that it is hardly surprising to me that we have seen such a devastating decline in our flora and fauna.

Diary excerpts:

7th August 1969: Weather slight wind hot sunshine and mist towards river Severn. Berwick woods hill. Many starling feeding on the ground (50 approx) 1 chaffinch near compound.

Blue tit in fir branches, male and female green woodpeckers flying over top field perching onto telegraph pole left side of field and on large elm tree at the bottom of the hill below the fir trees. Jay perched on dead tree making rasping call. Male and female black headed gull flying south east. No signs of grey squirrel in the woods. House martins and swallows flying over top field. Numerous flies and mosquitoes seen. Grass long and all blackberry bushes with flowers and rose hips.

25th May 1970 Hallen marsh. Weather warm slight breeze. A pair of green woodpeckers at (thought to be) nest sight in dead tree on corner of Hills field. Wrens nest in roots of a fallen tree behind ruin of Hills farm.

Male Reed bunting flying along ditch perching onto a willow. One heron flying west landing in bent tree. Grasshopper warbler seen and heard near farm in low scrub. A pair of redstarts in a ploughed field catching mosquitos. Pied flycatcher on the other side of the field. Heard a pheasant nearby. A mallard flew up from a rhine, circling then flying north.

Water vole jumped into the water as we passed near second railway arch. Found a chaffinch nest next to the railway on straight section of Moorhouse lane.

5th February 1971 Berwick woods. 7:30 p.m. No wind, warm, ground muddy. 1 badger observed at lower entrance on main sett. Activity heard in gully below. Smelt a fox in heath field. 2 tawny owls in the ponds area yelping and warbling??

The kestrel was a bird once commonly seen on my walks, known also as the *windhover* it mastered the air hovering almost motionless, hanging in the air over the long grass in its search for voles and mice, with quivering wing tips before dropping like a stone onto its prey. The kestrel population crashed in the eighties for some inexplicable reason, so we do not know how to avoid it happening again. Perhaps herbicides, the loss of long grassy meadows and thousands of miles of hedgerows could have something to do with this?

Occasionally I would see a handsome red fox with thick ginger tail, his brush, wandering quietly through the meadow on the lookout for food. Foxes have a varied diet not always described in the books, and include plants and even craneflies, which are a favourite in the autumn. Sick lambs and poultry can also be taken but they are not the preferred source of food if others are available. Foxes were often shot by farmers and gamekeepers who considered these animal a threat, but shotguns are inaccurate and often injure animals inflicting on them a slow painful death.

Any wild bird and animal during winters' bad weather will obviously seek easy sources of food, we lost some of our own chickens and ducks to the fox but I have always thought any animal, even vermin, still deserves respect and a quick and humane death. The fox in some places became a problem to livestock as a result of high fox numbers, a depleted natural wild food resource and no natural predator.

I seldom see foxes in the countryside today but the urban fox is very common and adapting to a semi-wild state in towns. They have even wandered into people's houses and bedrooms. I am not sure that is a good for the fox or the local human population.

Walks with the Dog

For as long as I can remember we always had a dog or two. I shared my childhood with Dorcas, she was a Collie cross Labrador and a few years later was joined by, one of her offspring we called Titch because it was the runt of the litter and we could not find a home for her. They both had to behave whenever out on walks. They were trained to stay quiet, kept close at heel and not to go out of sight when off the lead and we would be rewarded by a close encounter of an unsuspecting bird or mammal.

By the age of 12 I was spending time in the woods, sitting quietly under a tree with my 10x50 binoculars, a prized birthday present, I would wait quietly to see the resident wildlife slowly appear. On a good day when it was warm with little wind, the yaffling laugh of the green woodpecker filled the air, similar to sound of a kookaburra; it would echo through the wood as it flew across the hill with its dipping flight and land onto an ant hill where it would find its favourite food of red ants.

It hopped along the ground and I could see it using its long sticky tongue, which actually extends around the top of its skull increasing its length three-fold, it probed deeply into the fine earth of the anthills scattered all around the field. These old anthills have become a rare feature today and are a sign of valued permanent herb-rich grassland. Wild thyme often grows on top of these anthills. Once extinct from England, the Large Blue butterfly relies on a complex relationship between one species of red ant, wild thyme and the ant nurturing the egg stage of the butterfly inside its nest. Modern farming has removed anthills from many acres of land so this habitat has become very rare.

Most of the farmers around us were kind to their land and kept a mixture of cattle, sheep, pigs, chicken, geese and ducks, all kept in small fields, often with ponds in undisturbed corners. Thick hedges surrounding the fields were scattered liberally with mature trees including elm, oak, willow, ash, crab apple and many hawthorns with handsome broad crowns thick with white flowers in May.

Trees of varying sizes and ages were dotted randomly across the mosaic of fields connecting the small woods and spinneys to the network of ditches. Even dead sentinel trees remained standing for years with their bleached white carcasses standing out from the green of the surrounding vegetation. I remember playing in one large hollow tree that had fallen across a ditch, it made a perfect den.

A few ponies were kept in the apple orchards that were scattered around each farm. Although this was a timeless scene of rural tranquillity it was so close to a dramatically changing world just a few fields away.

I would go for walks often twice a day before and after school. I was free to explore this landscape and to follow my curiosity, seeing the natural world thriving around me, whether it was seeing an orb spider in her incredibly symmetrical engineered woven web or watching a buzzard soaring high above me and so rare at that time. This was the early and privileged introduction that I had to my natural environment. Dorcas and Titch both had a great time.

The floodplain of the Severn valley and surrounding landscape was still a fertile network of agricultural fields with deep ditches. Some of the fields were undulating with ridge and furrow, designed to be flooded and then drained to bring on early spring grass after the winter.

As well as water voles these waterways were home to sticklebacks, minnows, great crested and palmate newts, dark green diving beetles with a yellow band had a very aggressive larvae which sucked the life out of small fish and could give a painful nip, so we avoided putting it in our jam jars. I remember its Latin name, *Dytiscus marginalis*.

In spring and summer my brother, sister and friends often spent our evenings after school pond dipping for these and other water life.

I shall not forget the first time when I saw a graceful, long-legged, long-necked grey heron, fishing in one of these shallower ditches. It stood over a metre tall, motionless, watching for movement in the water, dagger beak at the ready. Most of these fields and ditches have largely disappeared under rugby playing fields, roads and warehousing.

In contrast to the low lying floodplain was Berwick Woods, which ran along a high ridge towards Spaniorum Hill. I have always thought Spaniorum was a delightful name for a piece of countryside. It was a mosaic of intimate fields and trees set on a plateau with oak and elm woodlands dissected by steep gullies exposing the deep red marl soil.

Spaniorum Hill was included in my grandfather's book and was described and designated as being "Remarkable Countryside" needing to be protected. It is still woodland and small fields as I remember it. Sadly the M5 motorway has sliced through the edge of this special place so what remains really deserves long-term protection.

Being rural (just) and still farming country, our village had few facilities (although more than some villages have today); a pub, garage, shop, a church and primary school. We made our own entertainment having hobbies making trolleys from pram wheels, riding bikes and horses, building dens and playing in the woods and fields.

Each summer the sound of the repetitive rhythm of the hay baler was heard well into the warm evenings, slicing and ramming the cut grass tightly together to make uniform lines of small, sweet smelling haybales. Before the grass was cut we used to make tunnels, crawling along on our bellies in the tall grass and buttercups, no doubt much to the farmers disapproval, but it was all part of our innocent growing up in the countryside.

Our walks each autumn was when mother put to us work again picking the blackberries and red rosehips hanging off the thick hedges flanking the quiet country lanes. Blackberry and apple pies and rosehip syrup were produced to last us for the next few months.

We seldom saw chemicals being spread or sprayed on the adjacent fields in the 1960s, the grass just grew after the dung was spread from the cattle sheds to produce a verdant sweet pasture of grass, with wild flowers and herbs for the animals to enjoy.

Gradually artificial fertilisers became more widespread as did land drainage schemes. The white granules of nitrogen fertiliser were spread liberally behind the tractors, dramatically changing the colour of the grass to an almost artificial deep green and the sward changed comprising of just a few grass species. Very little concern was voiced about this change, simply because we did not understand the implications of enriching our soil artificially when cheap food was needed at any cost.

As I grew up I think my moral compass came from neither the church nor from school but from having the responsibility for the animals I had to care for. My mother also taught me to respect my environment. This began early by being told never to drop litter.

We had around 15–20 animals at home and we all helped to look after them every day while also working on the local farms and it taught me to respect animals, not to be afraid of getting my hands dirty, and to use my common sense. The animals had to be fed and watered daily, some were exercised regularly and their sleeping quarters always kept clean and dry. I learnt from this that animals are a full-time commitment and that you cannot neglect them or go on holiday and leave them unattended.

Although we call ourselves a nation of animal lovers I have seen unnecessary cruelty and prolonged suffering by poor husbandry, showing little true regard for the animals' welfare. Treating them more like human beings and spoiling them with treats can result in unhappy and unhealthy animals.

CHAPTER 2

SCHOOL DAYS

I started school in the local primary school in the village but I did not enjoy my school days at all. As well as attending school I was also taken to church each Sunday. There was pressure from the family early on for me to conform and do well academically. My uncles and cousins were all professionals in engineering and medicine, so my mother also expected her offspring to follow a similar profession and have a successful career. Who can blame her?

After leaving the village primary school I had a good start to my education, attending a private school with the wonderful name of Compton Greenfield Preparatory school. Compton Greenfield was a small hamlet set in a valley below the earlier mentioned Spaniorum hill. The school was run by Mr and Mrs Harper and their two daughters and was just a couple of miles away from home, so in summer, we could walk to school along the quiet lanes lined with tall graceful elms that were all cut down in the seventies.

Nearly 50 years later, although much younger and smaller now, the elms are still growing along the lanes there today. Many have been spared the flail and allowed to grow up. Despite the presumption by many people that we had lost elms forever, this is an important lesson to heed and to not repeat the hasty removal of affected ash trees that are likely to be affected by ash die back disease in coming years. Even if some trees are affected we must retain valuable deadwood habitat that they will provide.

Back to my schooling, Compton Greenfield Preparatory school was far from being an orthodox centre of learning. The 60 pupils were mostly girls. Each week the few boys, about 12 of us, would be sent outside into the extensive grounds to do various maintenance tasks under the watchful eye of Mr Harper the maths teacher, while the girls did their ballet lessons indoors.

The boys were put to work and cut back vegetation, lit bonfires and I thoroughly enjoyed all this physical work. This was something I have always thought was far more worthwhile and inspiring than sitting indoors and being academic, learning algebra and obscure facts that seemed to me irrelevant.

I am sure that this early "education" had a great influence in my determination to work in the outdoors.

Suffice to say I failed the 11+ exam for messy writing or something equally trivial. This was much to my mother's disappointment and great angst and it sent me off on an unintended route that my parents tried their best to avoid. I

17

found myself a pupil at one of the most notorious secondary schools in the county, five miles distant from home. My mother tried to get me to attend a more respected senior school just a mile away from home instead, but without success.

The secondary school I attended for five long years was a grim introduction to the great big wild world and a very alien one to someone who was from the countryside. Many of the pupils and teachers lived amongst the urban sprawl of north Bristol.

Until 11 years old I had been rather short and fat in stature and was the shortest in the family but I was now growing quickly and was becoming quite tall and eventually outgrew my parents, my brother and sister. This did not help my introduction to this harsh new school environment because my father insisted that I continue to wear short trousers to school, amongst the rabble of smoking, swearing fellow pupils with broad Bristolian accents, all in their long trousers!

I was endlessly bullied and ridiculed because I spoke rather differently using English grammar as intended, with the absence of any colourful language. This was not helped by my inability to play any sport very well. I could not kick or hit a ball straight and I hated the idea of running headlong into an opponent to place an elongated ball between two white posts, a new game to me called rugby!

I often found myself standing on a freezing touch line because no one wanted me as a member of their team for football, rugby or cricket. I would occasionally be placed in the left back position or in goal for football, as a last resort, because I could reach the crossbar and I filled the space well.

There were times when I was embraced by my fellow classmates, this would be during school trips while doing projects. I was always put forward as the spokesperson to engage with the adults and ask questions to get information, which we all then used when writing up our projects about our visit.

In hindsight all these challenges helped to strengthen my character and determination. It taught me not to follow the herd or to give way to peer pressure. I actually preferred to be different and would often tell fellow pupils how I would venture out at night into the nearby woods at home to watch badgers.

My teachers were not very supportive either and seemed to want to demoralise me for having unorthodox interests that the school did not seem to recognise.

My three maths teachers were all very stern and I found the subject just hellish. Not having a mathematical brain was incomprehensible to them and they did not recognise that some people just did not find mathematics easy, you were thought to be thick, stupid or a combination of both!

However, I enjoyed English language and I was fluent at speaking French when I left my prep school, but was held back in the senior school because no one else had done French before. Geography and biology were fascinating subjects and I was good at them. We had some very interesting field trips to the Cotswolds and the Dorset coast.

A real confidence buster happened in my third year at

school, I enjoyed sketching and had spent a long time drawing wildlife in my own sketch pad at home when, surprisingly, I was told by my art teacher that as I could not draw still life subjects I should consider doing another subject. I was not willing to accept this decision so I showed the teacher the drawings that I had done at home and was then permitted to continue to study art. I achieved an O level in art.

My woodwork teacher also recommended that I should leave his class as well and to forget trying to make towel racks due to such poor joints that I cut. Later, during my career however I was to construct many things from wood, building cross country fences, aviaries, timber bridges and garden features from cleft timber.

The school was located in the north end of Bristol where I could see from the upper floors of the buildings the end of the Cotswold escarpment at Tog Hill. During many classes I would often yearn to be walking under the line of beech trees that I could see, or of taking my next walk with the dog, exploring woods or a new nature reserve.

In my spare time I would find every opportunity to learn about wildlife and to educate myself about the natural world and environment, something I thought was very important and so interesting to me.

Before we left school everyone had meetings with our career master, he was supposed to help me in advising on a career that suited me best. However when I told him of my aspirations to manage wildlife and the countryside, he informed me in a very matter-of-fact voice that I would never be paid for walking around fields and I should find a proper job instead with British Aerospace or Rolls Royce!

He gave a similar opinion to a class mate who was a farmer's son and he was a very good horseman, always winning rosettes at the gymkhanas, he was determined to pursue a career as a farrier, however the advice he got was that it was a dying trade and he should also join Rolls Royce!

That summed up the career advice we received and the knowledge, or lack of it, of countryside and environmental job sector. I should point out, that this was in the early 70's when it was becoming so much clearer then that we were seeing a significant impact on our wildlife and natural habitats. It was exasperating that no one else but me seemed to be aware of it.

I think this is an illustration of how confidence needs to be built up and not crushed when people are young and how important it is for teachers to give confidence and have belief in their student's natural abilities, to encourage them to follow their passion. If we had listened to his advice goodness knows what I would have finished up doing.

By the way Geoff became a well-respected farrier and established a successful business.

I believe that there is no substitute for practical experience so I am very pleased that apprenticeships are at last once again now considered that learning practical skills are a worthwhile alternative to studying for a degree.

Although at the time I left school no such apprenticeship existed in countryside management, I decided that by acquiring practical experience would be the best approach to carving out my chosen career while learning a fascinating subject.

My teachers gave me poor reports and had low expectations of my exam results at the time but I was able to acquire O level English language and Art and various CSE's including geography and biology, my two favourite subjects.

The irony was that the biology exam, which I passed, did not include many questions that covered subjects on what we had actually learnt in class. Luckily I had learnt most of it outside of school through my hobby! More about this later.

It is worth saying here that since leaving school in 1971 and despite the unhelpful guidance I received as a young and easily influenced lad, I have worked almost full time in the conservation sector or in a countryside job, with just a few brief spells when I needed to find other work.

I have also produced artwork for interpretation leaflets and panels for various wildlife sites.

CHAPTER 3

ENJOYING THE GREAT OUTDOORS

As we approached our teens my sister, brother and I had joined the guides, boy scouts and cub movements respectively. I loved the camping and hiking opportunities that it offered me to explore new countryside, many miles away from home and to use my initiative, learn to be innovative while camping; making ovens, rope swings and makeshift shelters and working alongside other people.

Back home in the woods we made bows and arrows from hazel stems although not realising at the time that the straight and springy spars we were cutting were the result of a once managed woodland that had been coppiced in the past.

The scouts also introduced me to working in small teams and the importance of working and rubbing along together, being respectful and diplomatic but also having a sense of humour at times, such as when the tent leaked at night and all the groundsheets were wet and the fire would not light in the morning.

As time went on I read more books and magazines including, the *Look and Learn* magazine and the very colourful *Birds of the World* publication with stunning photographs.

I collected many books on natural history (none of them on the school booklist). I spent time in the library where my mother worked for some years and in George's bookshop opposite the Bristol museum. I found the selection of books there was much more technical than just identification books on birds and general natural history and I remember buying *Black's Veterinary Manual* and the *Life of Mammals Volume 2*.

Opposite the bookshop at the top of Park Street was Bristol Museum, a place that I also explored to see the collections of animals from around the world in the enormous glass cases containing stuffed gorillas, antelope and even a giraffe, numerous birds from other continents and exotic islands in their splendid, if faded, plumage. I even took an interest in the art galleries exhibiting paintings of English landscapes on display there.

All this was largely a solitary occupation, and I had few real friends. I nevertheless enjoyed being independent and had become comfortable with my own company, enjoying my visits to the bookshops, the museum and walking the countryside with the dog.

I was joined sometimes by a friend of mine called Peter;

we were both members of the Bristol Naturalist Society and his father Desmond was a professional forester with the Forestry Commission, based at Westonbirt Arboretum in Gloucestershire.

When I first visited the arboretum I was stunned by the beauty and variety of this fine collection of trees from all around the world. It was a much quieter place then compared to today. This was where tree science is explored by the Forestry Commission (FC) who also maintained the beautiful trees that include colourful Japanese acers, rare conifers and exotic species of hardwoods.

The original trees were planted by Robert Holford and his son Sir George Holford. Robert Holford was a visionary and passionate plant collector and thanks to both their passion for trees, we can enjoy their legacy 130 years later. Westonbirt is a special and all too rare place to see the diversity of trees and appreciate the natural form of how trees grow as nature intended. Many are growing with low and broad canopies of branches by having the space that they need.

It is also a perfect example of how trees today can offer an environment for people as a place to relax and enjoy. Westonbirt has become a destination to visit by many thousands of people wanting to explore and enjoy trees. This is a big change from the days when tree boffins and foresters were the only visitors. Trees have become mainstream factor in our lives, at last.

Peter's father Desmond introduced me to these special trees and through his knowledge was a great inspiration to me and he always encouraged me to pursue my interest in trees and wildlife. He later tested me on my naturalist scout badge, which was one of few scout proficiency tests that I acquired. However, I never actually received it because a naturalist badge could not be found anywhere. So rarely was it taken then!

I remember one special day when Desmond took Peter and I on a journey all the way up to the Towie valley in mid-Wales in his Morris 1100. This was where the FC were busy planting a new conifer forest. We travelled for miles along newly formed stone tracks carved along the contours of the endless bare uplands. The open hills were all being ploughed in advance of the conifer trees being planted.

It was little appreciated then what the impact of this monoculture of spruce and pine trees in regimented rows would be. Forty years on we are seeing the acidification of water quality by these planting schemes and from tree diseases wiping them out. I was saddened then to see this wilderness being planted with so many alien trees. I remember asking Desmond why, but it was thought then to be the right thing to do.

While in the area we also went to look for what was at the time the very elusive and rare red kite. This is a bird of prey that was once common across London, they were later persecuted in Victorian times, fortunately a few found refuge in these wild hills of mid-Wales.

We did get a brief glimpse of a kite and heard its plaintive haunting siren call drifting across the distant hillside. This bird is now a common sight across southern England following reintroduction. I hope a sustainable population can become established, although I believe the continuing feeding of these birds may cause artificial numbers to survive, potentially causing an ecological imbalance.

Learning new skills.

Encouraged by my mother I joined the Bristol Naturalist Society. Their field trips took me to more interesting places around Gloucestershire and Somerset including nature reserves such as Wetmoor, Midger Wood and Crook Peak, where I learnt more about nature in its natural habitat by knowledgeable, informed and practical people who led the field these events. One person was Morley Penistone, a tall wiry gentleman full of interesting facts about the environment and always worth listening to.

I learnt to do live trapping of small rodents, using clever devices called Longworth traps. These were comprised of two metal tin sections connected together with a clip; one of the sections is a tunnel with a trapdoor activated by a treadle and the other larger section was the living quarters that would have bedding, some food including a piece of apple, to ensure whatever animal was caught could survive until being released.

After setting these traps we would return later that day or the next morning, to see what had been caught. Any small mammal we found in a trap would be carefully removed, decanting it into a plastic bag to weigh it. Knowing that they always run up hill helped to manoeuvre the animal easily in the bag. They were then released unscathed. This work went towards understanding what small mammals were actually living in the woods and what condition they were in.

I also spent time visiting and recording the birds that turned up at Chew Valley Reservoir and keeping records of the badger sett activity near my home as part of the Mammal Society national badger survey.

While still at school I joined the Conservation Corp which later became the British Trust for Nature Conservation Volunteers (BTCV). I went on weekend work parties to keep footpaths open and to maintain habitats on nature reserves that certain wildlife needed.

One morning when camping at the Wetmoor nature reserve, on emerging from the tent, I was greeted by a large selection of fungi foraged that morning from the woods by the Doc. He was an expert on fungi, I had only eaten a field mushroom before so, after some encouragement I enjoyed a hearty breakfast of interesting and colourful specimens such as beefsteak and parasol fungi. **Please do not try eating fungi without an expert choosing the goodies from the baddies first**.

It should also be noted that foraging, when done on an industrial scale to supply commercial food outlets, can do irreparable damage to fungal populations a result of the recent new fashion for wild food. Doc was another enthusiastic but older naturalist from whom I learnt a lot. He did a lot of good work for the Somerset Trust for Nature Conservation.

Nature Reserves. What have we learnt?

The late sixties, early seventies was time when the Wildlife Trusts and Natural England (what was then Nature Conservancy Council) believed the best way to conserve our wildlife was to acquire or purchase often small isolated blocks of woodland, heath or grassland with a rare habitat or species, which had been spared from modern agricultural or forestry practices. They made a gallant effort to protect these areas by putting a fence around them, and excluding livestock. The land history of each site however was often overlooked or unknown and this meant continuing the traditional management of the site ceased which was key to maintaining its character and diversity.

Sadly over time some sites became over grown by neglect because of the loss of traditional management and others increasingly isolated from similar sites by the adjacent intensive land use. This resulted in an impoverishment of species unable to move and maintain a rich gene pool of its populations, such as butterflies and bats, unable to reproduce or find food from enough foraging land. This also came at a time when we saw the beginning of much more intensive farming causing the steady decline and critical mass of plants, insect and bird populations across the wider countryside.

Modern agricultural practices has fragmented habitats and removed much of the feeding and foraging ground where plants and insects once happily survived.

*We have all learnt a lot since those days about ecosystems and the importance of understanding the **history** of a site, that a **larger habitat** is crucial to enable it to function and that its **connection to the wider landscape** to **maintain the critical mass** of species are all vital for their continuing resilience and survival.*

However we still know little about the very small and microscopic elements that are all vital components of a functioning, sustainable and resilient eco system.

Despite valiant attempts to conserve our flora and fauna, in 2017 it is still declining putting many species in an increasingly vulnerable and threatened state.

Maps and taxidermy.

By joining the scouts I was also able to enjoying hiking. I was taught how to read a compass and OS map and this showed me more places to explore. I became very interested in the maps, what they showed and how they were produced, learning the symbols revealed a story about the landscape of Gloucestershire. On older maps each tree and hedgerow were marked so we can see just how many across our landscape have been lost and not replaced.

I saved up enough from my paper round to purchase a large scale 25-inch map of the area around my village. It showed so much detail of a landscape that was already slowly disappearing. (I once considered becoming a cartographical surveyor when exploring career options, it was an outside job, but at the time I enquired, the Ordnance Survey only wanted draughtsmen in their offices but not surveyors.)

When I was 14 years old I won a Collins bird identification book as first prize in a competition for producing a hand drawn map of my local woodland, showing all the natural history that I had seen there. *A rare achievement for me to win anything.*

Maps also opened my eyes to the world beyond my village and I used to go for long cycle rides exploring new places on my second hand Dawes racing bike with engraved handlebars.

Using books to learn about nature are very useful but they should never be taken as being absolutely accurate when describing animal behaviour. Animals obviously have not actually read the books themselves so they often do things that the book does not mention or we know about! A pair of binoculars and a hand lens opens up a whole new world where you can always learn something new and to see, what to so many, is unseen and unappreciated.

I recall seeing the stuffed animals in Bristol museum and not being able to afford a specimen of my own so I taught myself from books how to taxidermise (preserve and stuff) dead animals and I also went to a demonstration by the resident taxidermist at the museum showing us the techniques of preserving skins and plumage and building an artificial body with wire and wood wool.

It was while still at school having boasted about the animals that I had found dead and stuffed already, that one of my school mates told me about a male heron that had been killed after flying into transmission wires. This bird was quite a challenge to skin and to preserve but I did succeed and it stood sentry in my bedroom for some years later. This was another reason why I suspect I was considered rather odd by my fellow classmates!

Using the bedroom as my workshop I finished up resurrecting numerous carcasses including a squirrel, a fox and head (mask) and much later some deer heads, but they never looked quite as nature intended again, so I gave up trying to do what is after all, a very skilled craft.

CHAPTER 4

CONTINUING DESTRUCTION CALLED PROGRESS

Witnessing changes in farming practice throughout my childhood and the developments causing destruction of the countryside around my home they became even more intense. The expansion of industrial complexes including ICI, British Gas and Rio Tinto zinc smelting company gobbled up green fields where we once walked. Our country walks became less enjoyable and it was obvious to me that the changes we were seeing were slowly sucking the life out of our landscape.

One lasting image has stayed with me. It was in 1969, I remember it all too well, when on one warm summer afternoon we were playing happily in a stream that cascaded down through our Berwick woods. We were making small mud and stone dams for the water to flow over when we heard a low droning sound above us up in the woodland getting louder and louder when eventually it crashed out of the trees pushing soil, whole trees and slabs of turf along with it.

Somewhat bewildered but also excited at the sight of this enormous yellow machine, a Caterpillar D8 bulldozer, I remember looking behind it into the wood and seeing an open gash of red marl soil ripped into the otherwise green, undisturbed woodland floor, the canopy broken and invaded for the first time by bright sunlight shining in from the sky above.

This was the start of the new M5 motorway around Bristol, a six-lane roadway destroying forever most of our woodland playground. This was just half a mile from home, and over the following months we watched thousands of tons of rock and earth removed as it sliced through our wooded hillside, destroying ancient oaks, the carpet of bluebells never to appear again in April and the woodland ravines filled in.

Fifty acres of land is used for every mile of motorway built.

A year later the middle part of the hillside had been completely removed by a fleet of scrapers and bulldozers, taking their loads of earth and rock on a journey south to build up the road on high embankments in the lower lying land.

If there was any good that came from this destruction, I did learn about the rocks and fossils that I discovered while exploring some of the piles of excavated material that was dumped on the hill above our village. It became a new place to explore (no fences or health and safety to worry about) and spend time to search out the fossils and learn about geology that revealed ammonites and other weird fossils that I had only seen once before on my school trip to the Dorset coast.

On one occasion I remember optimistically thinking that I had struck gold when I found small fragments of a shiny yellow mineral in the blue Lias clay. However when proudly showing my mother, she soon disillusioned me and informed me that I had found Copper pyrites, otherwise known as fool's gold.

Today when I drive between Cribbs Causeway and Portbury on that motorway I feel guilty using it because it is so sad to know what the countryside was like before it was carved up. Along the margins of the motorway I see just horses grazing in featureless fields now with a few stunted trees framing an industrial landscape behind.

At the same time the motorway was being built in the late sixties, our local narrow country lanes were also widened, the large dead and dying elm trees were being felled and sapling that were trying forlornly to regrow were uprooted (there was no interest in replacing the trees). Miles of hedges were being ripped out across farmland across England, so too the scattered older trees in the fields that had stood there for centuries. Their spreading boughs gave shelter to animals but were systematically removed to make farming "easier" and more "efficient". The ditches around us were straightened and cleared of trees and vegetation. This was called flood protection at the time!

This all payed for by the taxpayers with more grants for acres of fields across the country to be land drained with long tubes of plastic piping; when countless ponds were filled in. I believe this has resulted in a drier desiccated soil which is unattractive to wildlife. Just see the biodiversity that is to be found around ponds, wetlands and rivers compared to drier areas.

Looking in my diary for 1970, I read that I was often seeing water voles in a part of Hallen called the marsh. These animals were once common in our waterways and wetlands. They were often seen along places like Moorhouse Lane sitting on the stream bank eating a blade of grass before plopping into the water. This lane ran parallel with the brook where numerous nest holes punctuated the steep banks. Water voles are a small aquatic mammal that have become very rare today. Pollution, the loss of bank side habitat and the thoughtless release of mink from fur farms in the 1980s have conspired to see the vole population crash by 90%.

Seeing the blue flash of the Kingfisher was another really special event to glimpse around these rhines and ponds. I got to know the best places to watch this beautiful bird as it flew low and straight as an arrow along the brook, stopping to perch on a branch before dipping quickly into the water and back to its perch. These birds had favourite flight lines and used them regularly around the same time of day, so it would be possible to sit and wait and be rewarded with a streak of turquoise blue darting along just above the water accompanied by a piping call. Much later in the 1990s when as head warden, I was to take children in London to see this same spectacle along the River Wandle.

In the 1970s on the nearby railway embankment the

grasshopper warbler and skylark were also regular birds heard more often than seen in summer, trilling out their distinctive calls, nesting and feeding in brambles and long tussocks of grass, perfect habitat.

Since I left Hallen yet another motorway, the M48, has been constructed across this part of the marsh as well as warehousing and new roads have surrounded the village!

CHAPTER 5

UNDERSTANDING THE BIGGER PICTURE

When I left school at 16 I had a driving ambition to work for nature and keep the world a biodiverse and richer, healthier place worth living in. Having already witnessed so much destruction and change in the countryside it set me off along a most interesting career journey over 47 years ago to follow a profession that I have continued to travel.

I am using my acquired knowledge and experience to keep fighting for a better environment for people and where the nature can also thrive.

My ambition has always been to play a small part in trying to stem the frightening irreparable damage and rate of change that is occurring across our landscape, by standing up for the natural world.

Unfortunately so far conservationists, politicians,

scientists, farmers, foresters, planners, and many land owners have not worked well together but instead have operated in separate "boxes" and it has not succeeded in conserving our natural environment, or maintaining a sustainable quality of life.

We all need to come up with a fresh approach, become wiser and to work a lot harder together.

Before the conservation of species or the regeneration of landscapes can be successful we need to know our land use history. We need to learn from our mistakes and recognise the bad choices that have been made, some regrettably are still being made, regarding our environment and management of our wildlife.

I was once told by a carpenter:

"The person who never makes a mistake learns nothing.
But the person who learns from their mistakes becomes wise"

The Importance of learning the right things

I think the following account is very relevant and worth telling.

As mentioned earlier, while at school and when taking my biology exam it included questions about farming that we had not been taught about in class! These questions were about pests and chemicals, i.e.:

Question: Name three wildlife species that are harmful to farmers?

Question: Name three chemicals used on farms that have affected British wildlife and explain why?

The three animals were: rabbit, mink and fox. The chemicals were: DDT, Dieldrin and Aldrin.

Luckily as explained earlier I did know the answers because I had learnt about it myself through my interest in the environment.

Although used for years in the countryside many people were, and are still today, quite unaware of the existence of these chemicals. My urban classmates were equally uninformed and had little knowledge of the countryside or how it was managed and wildlife was being destroyed around them.

Just a few of my fellow pupils, including Geoff and another farmer's daughter, were able to get a good biology exam result, largely due to our farming background and my own self learning about the threats to wildlife in the sixties. I had also learnt about the natural environment *outside* of school.

This episode strengthened my scepticism about the shortcoming of purely academic education and the disadvantage of remembering answers to questions for just passing exams. The more exams you pass today the better the schools and politicians like it. It appeared to me that being able to get a good score to pass exams is a rather shallow form of learning.

To remember facts to pass an exam on just one day of your life is not, in my opinion, proper education. However to acquire knowledge about many things and understand how they relate and impact on each other is far more important.

I include the following information to remind us of what we need to be aware of but have ignored, forgotten or were never told.

Dieldrin is a chemical produced as a pesticide. It was widely used by the agriculture industry during the 1950s until early 1970s.

Despite concerns by ecologist at the time who were finding deformed wildlife and many young animals found dead, this chemical continued to be used in GB and America up until the early seventies, and it is probably still being used in some parts of the world today.

Regardless of this history we are continuing to use chemicals on our food and crops including neonicotinoid, which it has been proven to damage bee populations and invertebrates. We also use glyphosate which is thought to be carcinogenic.

How might Dieldrin affect the environment?
Internet Info.

Dieldrin is highly toxic to aquatic organisms and many other forms of wildlife and it can accumulate in the environment, particularly in the fat of animals. Dieldrin binds strongly to soil particles and is not easily broken down. Little seeps to ground waters. That which evaporates from soils into the atmosphere may travel considerable distances before being re-deposited elsewhere. Dieldrin is classed as a "persistent organic pollutant" (POP). The effects of Dieldrin pollution cause concern at a global as well as local level. [SOURCE,

SEPA,http://apps.sepa.org.uk/spripa/Pages/SubstanceInform
ation.aspx?pid=39]

This is what we happily spread across our landscape to grow
better food!

Scientists are often heralded as intelligent but when we
use science to justify carrying out short-sighted
environmental destruction we must always challenge
decisions and practices in the name of efficiency and for
growth driven by politics and economics.

One other chemical we once relied on, thinking it was the
perfect answer to crop diseases was DDT.

DDT was one of the first chemicals in widespread use as
a pesticide. Following World War II, it was promoted as a
wonder-chemical, the simple solution to pest problems large
and small. Today, nearly 40 years after DDT was banned in
the US, we continue to live with its long-lasting effects:

- **Food supplies:** USDA found **DDT breakdown
  products** in 60% of heavy cream samples, 42% of kale
  greens, 28% of carrots and lower percentages of many
  other foods.

- **Body burden:** DDT breakdown products were found in
  the blood of 99% of the people **tested by CDC**.

- **Health impacts:** Girls exposed to DDT before puberty
  are five times more likely to develop breast cancer in
  middle age, according to the **President's Cancer
  Panel**.

- Banned for agricultural uses worldwide by the 2001
  **Stockholm Convention on Persistent Organic
  Pollutants,**

The author Rachel Carson highlighted the dangers of DDT in her ground-breaking 1962 book *Silent Spring*. Carson used DDT to tell the broader story of the disastrous consequences of the overuse of insecticides, and raised enough concern from her testimony before Congress to trigger the establishment of the Environmental Protection Agency (EPA).

Her work attracted outrage from the pesticide industry and others. Her credibility as a scientist was attacked, and she was derided as "hysterical," despite her fact-based assertions and calm and scholarly demeanour. Following the hearings, President Kennedy convened a committee to review the evidence Carson presented. The committee's review completely vindicated her findings.

One of the new EPA's first acts was to ban DDT, due to both concerns about harm to the environment and the potential for harm to human health. There was also evidence linking DDT with severe declines in bald eagle populations due to thinning eggshells. Since DDT was banned in the US bald eagles have made a dramatic recovery.

History Repeating? Recently, Carson's work has again been targeted by conservative groups. Capitalising on the iconic status of DDT, these groups are promoting widespread use of the chemical for malaria control as part of a **broader effort to manufacture doubt** about the dangers of pesticides, and to promote their anti-regulatory, free market agenda while attempting to undermine and roll back the environmental movement's legacy.

Many DDT promoters are also in the business of denying climate change.

Attacks on Carson from groups like the Competitive Enterprise Institute and Africa Fighting Malaria **portray DDT as the simple solution** to malaria, and blame Carson for "millions of deaths in Africa." Many of these **DDT promoters** are also in the business of denying climate change and defended the tobacco industry by denying the health harms of smoking.

A recent report in 2017 by EU assessing the impact of pesticides and herbicides has stated that they can affect our mental health and IQ. That they can also cause cancer, diabetes and Parkinson's disease. Organic food production is therefore much healthier.

It is more than worrying that we still seem to have a similar mindset today on the reliance on chemicals for food production and also promoted in America with the new administration, pursuing a similar agenda in 2018 of denying global warming and relying on fake news!

Rachel Carson, was eloquent and correct about environmental concerns in *Silent Spring*. Rainforests were and continue to be felled and in 1967 the Torrey Canyon oil tanker devastated our coastline having become shipwrecked on the Cornish coast and spilling thousands of tons of crude oil along miles of coast. One of the many spills around the globe, killing untold numbers of birds and marine life.

To put this in context, over the last 50 years, a relatively short time, I have seen countryside either disappear or many thousands of acres become degraded across the British isles, yet we continue to be dependent on the use of oil and chemicals to produce food.

The Soil Association has highlighted that despite a ban on neonicotinoids since 2013, almost a quarter of British honey samples are still contaminated and new research shows common fungicides are linked to steep bumblebee declines.

Although there is no safe dose of a toxic chemical there has been an increase in the use of different chemicals on three crops in the UK Onions X18 chemicals, wheat X12 chemicals, potatoes X6 chemicals.

Despite clear messages being learnt from previous bad practices, threats to our health and ecological destruction still continue. It confirms the real concerns I had when just 11 years old and which are even more relevant today.

We need to make big changes very soon.

CHAPTER 6

MY JOURNEY BEGINS

Native otters were very rare in our rivers in the late 1960s and David Chaffe had set up a small wildlife park devoted to British wildlife conservation just two miles from my home. While still at school I would make regular visits there to draw the animals and enjoy their company.

I left school at lunch time on July 5th 1971 and started my working life that afternoon in this wildlife park. David and his wife Jane were both passionate if eccentric people and they were determined to follow in the late Sir Peter Scott's footsteps. He had opened the park to raise awareness about wildlife and the need to stop further environmental damage and species going extinct.

Some weeks before leaving school, and intent on beginning my career working with wildlife, I had contacted David and he agreed to give me an informal interview in the shop at the entrance to the park. The room smelt of fishmeal, bird food and dogs. I obviously convinced him then that I was worth employing for £9 per week because he asked me to start as soon as possible.

David often appeared on television with the late Johnny Morris on the BBC *Animal Magic* programme with his otters or some other wild animal.

All the animals and birds at the park were kept in relatively large enclosures in semi-natural surroundings. There were just two of us doing the day-to-day work, with the help of Jane. I worked with Denzil from Yorkshire and my job was to help provide the everyday needs of all the animals, about 200 altogether. These included two golden eagles, four eagle owls, ravens, a family of red and fallow deer, two roe deer, two Scottish wildcats, foxes, badgers and otters, and numerous ducks and geese usually found around our shores. We also had families of both Atlantic and Common seals, some coypu (that are not native), three gannets, six raven and many birds of prey. Some were trained to the wrist and would sit on their blocks on the lawns being admired by visitors. We took some of these animals around to schools, WIs, and they also often appeared on television.

The work was always very varied making it so interesting. In the morning after feeding time we would build or repair paths and steps around the enclosure and aviaries. We erected fences and cleaned out the seal pools and then took school groups around the animals or made an evening trip in the minivan to attend an evening talk to a WI or Rotary club, sharing the small space with two badgers and a buzzard or kestrel.

Despite well-known advice never to work with children or animals we did both on a daily basis. We were invited to attend many publicity events with animals including one with the 1969 Miss World. She was Miss Eva Von Staier and was promoting a raffle being run by Volkswagen and World Wildlife Fund for Nature, WWF. We regularly took animals to the local television studios. I gave a television interview with a kestrel on my wrist on a programme called *Women Only*. On another occasion we were asked to take a seal to promote a swimming pool then having to retrieve the seal from the pool that had been erected outside the Victoria rooms at an Ideal Home exhibition in Bristol.

To catch the seal I had to borrow a pair of one of the attendant lady's model bikini pants, which attracted quite a few onlookers to watch the spectacle to retrieve the seal. I waded into the pool and eventually persuaded it back into the crate while trying to retain my dignity... just!

Many schools visited the wildlife park, it was a valuable education resource for city dwellers and children who could get close up to the many native species that they otherwise would never see because they had become so rare or extinct in the wild!

The following year we had senior schools and the teachers who were particularly keen for the pupils to learn about their native wildlife and the threats they faced from agriculture, so I found myself teaching classes of children, just a year younger than me, about chemicals used on farms and about unsustainable farm practices. Strange that a few months earlier I was asked to explain these very things in my own biology exam! Life throws up strange twists of fate from time to time.

Sadly and all too often we saw the proof of the damage caused from the chemical sprays that were then widely used. While working at the park, birds of prey were often found by the public and brought into us, suffering from the effect of pesticides and other unknown chemicals. A badger was found one day semiconscious in a garden and was thought have eaten slug pellets. Some sprays caused deformed limbs and wings, many egg shells were too thin and broke on laying. Most of these casualties had little chance of recovery and were destroyed.

On a more positive side I really enjoyed being able to introduce visitors to the healthy animals, including some birds of prey that I trained for falconry. The bird would sit on my wrist and I would fly a kestrel or a buzzard attached to a long leash called a cre'ance.

This displayed the flying and hunting skills and showed the birds specialised attributes, their strong talons, hooked beak and enormous eyes, all at close quarters. To train these birds was a great lesson for me in patience. It would take weeks of sitting with the bird to acquire the birds trust and show them that I was their only source of food. Eventually I could get the bird to sit on a post then walking about 60 feet away, I raise my fist holding a day old chick, the bird would bob its head focussing on its reward with eyes transfixed, before flying gracefully wings outstretched, landing with a thud onto a leather gauntlet covering my hand and wrist. It would jealously guard its food by spreading out its wings to cover its catch as it ripped it apart.

The diet for all the meat eaters at the park included these dead, day old chicks, that we collected from a hatchery; these were the cock birds, which were worthless commercially for egg production but were very nutritious for our many hungry carnivores. Other food we used included frozen fish for the seals and a range of cereals, vegetables and dry cake foods for the deer and other herbivores.

We fed the seals each afternoon when the visitors would congregate anxiously around the pools and watch the seals come to life after lying quietly around the enclosure on small gravel beeches. They would torpedo through the water rising out of the water to catch a fish in their mouth as it was thrown in their direction; this was followed closely by a bow wave that broke over the attentive onlookers. All great fun.

Being in captivity and not able to choose their food, trace elements were vital part of the animals diets and was given with the fish via powder or pills such as kelp and linseed oil to keep their fur, skin and vital organs in good condition.

While at the park I hand reared a number of abandoned animals including badgers, deer, a fox and a Soay ram called Marmaduke, some of these were hidden under my trenchcoat and taken home on the bus before putting to bed in my bedroom until they were old enough to survive 24 hours without food!

I met a young lady called Dee who regularly used the bus as well and she became very interested in the work I did, her boyfriend Nick was a keen photographer and he spent a day with me taking pictures of the animals with great results.

Despite all this early attention, it is important for wild animals to stay wild and not become imprinted on you. As wild animals mature sexually many become instinctively territorial, even when in captivity. Some animals can become dangerous if hand reared as they lose the fear of man but retain their natural hormonal urges. Badgers and deer are just two that I was to see the consequences of this.

A man in Scotland was killed by a Roe deer buck when he returned home late from a wedding wearing strange smelling clothes. Forgetting to give the customary whistle to a hand reared rutty, territorial buck in the garden he was attacked and killed. The deer's speed and devastating injuries from sharp antlers can easily cause fatal injuries.

Phil Drabble, a BBC wildlife commentator, lost some toes when he ventured into his tame badger enclosure at the wrong time and was set upon by a territorial boar.

Although I was never a fan of wild animals in close captivity, the animals in the park were all kept in large natural enclosures and seemed largely content and healthy. Some had injuries having survived illegal trapping and given to the park so could not be returned to the wild.

These animals, all native in the UK served an invaluable role in raising awareness about our natural world at home. The wildlife park was an important and rare local resource available to the public and to schools in Bristol, to obtain a unique experience they would cherish and remember.

I think all the visitors to the park and those who attended one of our many talks will have learnt something new about their native wildlife and have become a little the wiser about their importance and the threats they face.

It was also a golden opportunity to remind people to respect our wildlife and that we must conserve and enhance their habitats.

It is depressing that the conservation profession was considered then and perhaps still is today, to be a quirky vocation confined for the weird and less intelligent. In the seventies I remember the schools considered it very odd for people to have any interest in planting trees or caring for your environment. At last this is changing but we still have a long way to go.

So it is heartening that natural world is much more appreciated today. Strangely however we continue to have a fascination for the rare species and not the common everyday wildlife around us. Why are we most interested in the species that are about to disappear? We must appreciate all nature whether common or rare.

We all grow up in or near to a countryside that is in a state of continuous change and modification so could this be why so many take it for granted and treat it with such contempt, having less and less contact with it but assuming it will always be there.

If so, then we could not be more mistaken.

CHAPTER 7

THE INFLUENCE OF HORSES AND DEER

In my teens I had an obscure physical condition which caused pain in my hips and prevented me from riding horses, something I had enjoyed from an early age. After numerous X rays over a few years it was thought the problem was caused because I had grown too fast and the hip joints had grown unevenly. The specialist surgeon suggested at the time the way to cure the problem would be to spend a year in bed or have an operation and reduce my activity!

I declined both treatments as it was just around that time when I was about to leave school to embark on my career.

So instead of riding horses in my spare time, I spent that time helping out at the local horse events, building cross country fences for hunter trials and then later for one-day horse trials. This meant working outdoors in lovely surroundings and was very satisfying, making solid structures out of tree trunks and using the landscape to create a challenge to horse and rider.

Later while still working at the wildlife park I was introduced one evening to Colonel Frank Weldon the director of Badminton international horse trials. Molly, another passionate horse woman and friend of my mother had invited him to a riding club drinks party. He kindly agreed to show me how he designed and built the fences for the famous three-day event which were much larger and more solid than anything I had built.

I would spend my day off each week through that winter and the early spring in the beautiful parkland of Badminton estate and I worked with the small fencing team from Willis Bros. They gave me an insight into their construction techniques, including the deft use of chainsaws, to create rustic masterpieces which they continue to do today over 40 years later.

To build the fences large conifer trees were cut from the nearby woodland for the upright posts and cross bars and sometimes used complete storm blown trees and perched them on a raised piece of ground to look even bigger. All the fences were solid constructions and well crafted. They were all strategically placed and carefully spaced apart to challenge the skill and courage of horse and rider.

Despite Colonel Weldon being very busy man organising the whole three-day event, he still found time to take me around the course in his Morris 1000 or Land Rover and explain the psychology behind building his unique and challenging fences that were intended to frighten the rider but gain the respect of the horse.

I learnt the importance of creating a balanced but challenging course and how to build a bounce fence by knowing the length of a horses stride. Although I no longer rode a horse I was still able to build courses which rode well. Locating a fence on a brow was one way of making the fence look much larger and where overhanging trees shaded a fence, it was important to consider the position of the sun during the competition.

While at Badminton I was given an opportunity, again arranged by Colonel Frank, to be interviewed by the Badminton estate manager because I expressed my interest in working on the estate, ideally with the deer, but no vacancy was available at the time.

I am sure working in that historic parkland focussed my determination to find a job where I could work in such beautiful surroundings while having a few deer to look after as well.

At the wildlife park in Bristol we had 17 deer altogether, they included an orphaned red deer stag from isle of Aran called Sannox and his three hinds, two fallow bucks with four does, a roebuck and doe, three Chinese water deer and later a pair of muntjac.

Mike was our deer adviser and a professional stalker and he made regular visits to the wildlife park to advise us on deer issues. He had a small herd of fallow deer in Ashton Court Park where a balloon festival is held these days.

A few months after I had started at the park as autumn

was arriving, Mike was called in because we had a problem. We had to deal with a dangerous fallow buck for the reasons mentioned earlier about tame animals and the territorial dominance of male deer. A dark brown fallow buck had now become sexually mature and rutty and was too aggressive for anyone to enter its enclosure.

At this time of year the deer come into rut, which means the animals become charged up with testosterone so having no fear of man, it had become intent on guarding its territory, and human beings were treated the same as any other deer. This can be very dangerous for anyone who has to work with them or if the public was to come into close contact with a deer like this.

Mike explained that the only way we could deal with this problem was unfortunately to despatch (shoot) the buck.

We had to wait for the right time to do this. A few days later, very early on a cold October morning, I cycled over to the park, both dreading what was to happen but also intrigued to witness the proceedings.

Mike had arrived armed with a high-velocity rifle and we walked in silence up to the enclosure. Before I realised it, he had shot the animal. The sound of the high velocity .243 rifle was deafening, the percussion of the shot knocked me backwards and left my ears ringing.

Mike then took me through the process of bleeding and gutting (gralloching) the animal as the carcass would not be wasted but would supply good venison meat.

(The wild cats in the park were given the lungs and stomach.)

This was a significant moment for me as before this event I could not contemplate the killing of wild animals. I remember seeing foxes injured with shotguns and caught in snares, so this was a lesson for me to appreciate that some animals, when necessary, do need to be destroyed or put down but it must be done humanely.

It would have been far too risky to leave the buck to injure the public, or worse but it also made me question if the animal should have been kept at the park in the first place.

Some months earlier Mike drove David and me in a soft top Land Rover all the way up to Woburn deer estate in Bedfordshire to purchase some deer for the park. My introduction to Woburn estate impressed me as much as did my visits to Badminton and it introduced me again to deer park management on another beautiful estate but on a much grander scale. Woburn is probably the largest deer estate in the country and had over 2000 deer, of nine species and was what remained of a larger animal collection established by 14th Duke of Bedford.

We were given a tour around the estate before we returned to Bristol with a few small deer in crates that David was keen to obtain for the collection. We had captured them with nets from a circular paddock and as we drove home I was unable to stop thinking just how special it would be to work at Woburn.

Following the Woburn visit and the fallow buck shooting incident, I had become even more interested in the deer at the wildlife park. I greatly enjoyed taking food to the deer in the early mornings. Most of them were free to run around the park until rutting time and they were fed under a small copse of beech trees. They got to know me and my usual call at feeding time.

After spreading the food in a line along the ground I would move just far enough away so they were able to eat undisturbed, but ready to react to any threat. They liked a regular routine but always remained wary and vigilant, highly strung and like a piece of elastic, ready to spring away at any sudden noise or movement back into the undergrowth.

I would sit quietly, watching and hearing them eat, watching their large ears constantly moving, their dark eyes alert and their tails twitching as they ate. The food was swallowed quickly to be regurgitated later and chewed again when quietly resting under cover. Being so close to them I could smell the pungent scent of the animals secreted from the numerous glands around their bodies.

Remarkably this scene was being played out in a quiet valley on the urban fringe of Bristol with the distant hum of rush hour traffic. Two very different worlds.

To prevent any further problems with the other male deer, Sannox, as the red stag had become bigger and stronger, Denzil and I had to assert our dominance by basically fighting with him to keep us at the top of the pecking order and maintain his respect so that we could enter his enclosure during the rut.

I feared in the end that eventually, as Sannox became too big, strong and dangerous, he would also probably have to be culled.

Lessons learnt:

We should always carefully consider the real benefits of keeping wild mammals in artificial and enclosed spaces. While zoos and wildlife parks do still play a valuable role in education, conserving rare and endangered animals, the animal's welfare must always be paramount consideration for their the best long term management.

However because humans in Britain have been such a major influence for centuries in the landscape and on our fauna and flora, perhaps we should be thinking of new and alternative ways to manage land for both food production and for natural biodiversity. Experimental work is being done to manage land more extensively, to even re-wild some places by moving away from traditional farming processes. This is already showing interesting results, such as at Knepp Estate, an ambitious project to manage land extensively and that we can all learn from and perhaps adopt some of their management principles and practices more widely.

Developing passion for deer

Seeing the deer every day at the wildlife park, I became increasingly respectful of them and in their ecology, the speed that their antlers grew each year just days after shedding the previous year's growth. Their eyesight and sense of smell is so acute. I learnt their ability to detect human scent with a favourable wind, from a mile or more away (even further if you wear aftershave), their acute hearing able to hear the slightest rustle or twig snap from perhaps up to quarter a mile away. Deer have glands all over their body, under their eyes, on their forehead and on their rear lower legs that they use to mark twigs and trees around their territory and send messages to other deer.

Deer are also physically incredibly strong animals, able to survive major injuries and are resistant to or able to survive many diseases that domestic animals suffer from. They combine graceful elegance with power, easily able to leap over six foot high fences from a standstill. I was to learn later that even when under the influence of strong tranquilisers they continue to be a challenge when being handled.

In contrast to this physical strength, they are mentally very highly strung and can sometimes just drop dead from stress. Deer are unique in the animal kingdom because the males grow antlers. These are often mistaken for horns – which are made from keratin that is hair – when antlers are made of solid bone.

Even more amazing is that the males (and females in reindeer) shed their antlers each year and grow a new larger pair each year. To produce such large structures is an incredible investment in energy. As the animal becomes mature after enjoying a number of breeding years, the antlers begin to grow smaller, affecting its dominance in the herd. Grown during the months between March and August, antlers sprout from a bony pedicles on the skull and grow rapidly – the antlers are fed by blood vessels by an outer skin of velvet. This sadly is an aphrodisiac prized by the Chinese.

Once the antlers are fully grown the blood vessels dry up, the velvety skin dies and is rubbed off on low branches. The antler is very dense bone, just try cutting it. The volume of bone grown by the older deer is equivalent to growing a pair of human thigh bones, in just a couple of months. Once the rut is over the hormone activity subsides and the following spring the antlers simply fall off and another pair begin to grow immediately.

It is still unclear precisely why the antlers are grown every year and is in sharp contrast to permanent horns grown by other animals such as antelope and cattle.

Being cast each year antlers were probably the first resilient material easily obtained by earliest man to be used as a tool. Picks made of antler have been excavated dating back to 5000 BC. Deer have played a key part in man's survival and development, not only is the meat very lean and healthy but skins and its leather, tendons, stomach linings and teeth were all were put to good use.

Berkley deer park safari

While still living and working in Bristol I spent some spare time at another deer park that Mike managed north of the city, so I was able to get to know him better and share his interest in deer while I helped him to manage the large herds of red and fallow deer that have roamed the park for centuries.

Each Friday evening I would meet Mike and his wife in Bristol during that autumn and winter and we would drive in his Land Rover out of Bristol, up the A38, and across the ancient park along deep rutted tracks. Finally arriving shaken and a little stirred, we reached our destination, an old cottage at the far end of the park. It was built into the deer park wall so the deer were literally in our back yard.

On our arrival I would soon be put to work to cut firewood and put life back into the log fire which warmed the house and which we later sat around, having eaten a delicious pre-prepared supper of venison or game pie, followed by some whisky.

The crackling flames and glowing embers warmly illuminated the room, helped by candlelight. I listened to Mike for hours reminiscing about his previous exploits with deer and his involvement in the SOE during the war, this was when he learnt how to survive on exercises in the highlands and had become intrigued by the deer which he also had to shoot for food.

One particular day at the park Mike returned from an early morning stalk with an ashen face and after a cup of tea recounted a pursuit of a fallow buck that had a long length of wire netting attached to its antlers. He lost sight of the deer as it entered a wood and he was then distracted when he came across a sick deer in front of him. As he lay on the ground to get ready to shoot this animal, on squeezing the trigger he felt something move under him and he was sent flying into the air, thinking for a moment that his gun had exploded.

Gathering his thoughts he looked around him and saw the original deer buck with the wire attached, running off at speed. Mike had been so close to the animal with the wire entangled on his antlers that he was actually lying on the wire just feet from the animal itself. As he took aim and shot the other deer the noise frightened the buck pulling Mike off the wire as it fled. This shows how deer will stay lying tight in the undergrowth to avoid being discovered.

Mike was a mysterious and quite secretive man and he never really let his guard down, but his passion for deer was always apparent and he taught me so much.

The 400-acre deer park at Berkley ran along a ridge and down to the river Severn flood plain which it overlooked to the west and across to the Cotswold escarpment in the east. It had been a deer park for many years and was enclosed by a high brick wall in the 19th century. Large veteran oaks with low, wide spreading branches, some touching the ground, were scattered across the grassland which was dotted with ant hills. This historic landscape with views across the Severn was intruded only by a nuclear power station. A solid square monolith stood out from the flat land and dominated the otherwise verdant network of fields and hedges running down to the grey waters of the River Severn. Although decommissioned recently, the concrete reactor core structure will remain as a blot on the landscape for centuries into the future.

The herds of red and fallow deer graze on the acid grassland, acorns and low growing foliage from the trees. Despite the poor nutrition available to the deer, they still grew well and strong, producing good organic meat. The ones that became weak, sick or suffered from injuries would be culled to prevent suffering and maintain the health of the overall herd, even during very bad weather. Long harsh winters are when, if there are too many deer, it can see many die from starvation unless supplementary feeding is given.

This scene around the park has remained unchanged for centuries where deer have grazed peacefully under the oaks with the sound of calves and fawns calling out to their mothers in summer. The park takes on a more primeval feel in misty autumns when the rut begins and the cold days and nights echoed with the roar and bellowing of stags and bucks.

This is a truly magical place sitting under an old oak tree, listening to and watching the seasonal changes playing out in front of me. It felt to me to be a place where I belonged.

This was another experience that made me decide to concentrate my next career move to learn more about these graceful beasts and their management.

On a recent visit back to the park I was pleased to see new oaks being planted and the plantations of pine and larch slowly being replaced with native trees to maintain the character of this ancient landscape.

CHAPTER 8

THE WOBURN DEER EXPERIENCE

Having tried to find work at Badminton without success and remembering my day trip to Woburn the previous year, I thought it would be a good place to enquire for a job being one of the largest deer parks in Britain. I wrote a letter to the estate office and by good fortune was invited along to an interview. This was at a time when you did not wait for an advert in the national press but had to use your initiative to find jobs. I am sure you can still do this today.

I thought the key qualities of getting work were: to be well mannered, hardworking, honest and trustworthy, to convince the employer of your dedication and interest and in return for obtaining useful practical skills and experience.

The day of my interview I was driven up to the park in Bedfordshire by my father who I never actually got on with or ever really understood. Spending his time in the pub after work he was not an attentive father and rather neglected the family as we grew up. He seemed bitter about life and very unwilling to play his role of being a father for reasons I never knew.

A car mechanic by trade, we had nothing at all in common. He did not support my interest in wildlife but I think on this rare occasion he felt he should help me out and at least get me to the interview. Although he was very sceptical about my chosen vocation, to give him credit, he delivered me to the door of Bedford Settled Estates in Woburn Park on a very misty day in November in 1972.

I was interviewed by the Estate Steward, as he was called, who managed the estate for the Marquis of Tavistock, owner of Woburn Abbey and surrounding 3000 acres. Mr Wiseman was an archetypal land agent. I remember the oak panelled office wreaked of cigar smoke. The Head Deer Keeper, Dennis Talbot was also at the interview.

Although I actually knew very little of what the work really entailed at the time I decided to take the job. I suppose it was gut instinct that I thought this was a good next step in my career.

Before returning to Bristol I was recommended by Mr Talbot to call in to an address in Woburn village where digs could be available. This was an old cottage, the oldest on the High Street and it had a sign outside; Registrar for Births, Marriages and Deaths!

Mrs Goodwin answered the door, she was an elderly lady in her seventies and she resembled Mrs Brown the comedian.

She was very friendly and took me in for chat. We sat in a small sitting room with large table and a loud television blaring out watched by an even older lady half asleep, stooped in an armchair. I was informed that a room was available but I would need to share. My enthusiasm to take the job and limited experience of life saw me agree to take up the offer, this would be introducing me to an unknown domestic situation that I had not experienced before.

Having agreed to take the room, we returned to Bristol and I recall being asked by my father, why on earth I should want to do such an odd job and live away in digs?

Back in Bristol I explained to my boss David of my decision to leave the park which he understood and wished me well, so I moved up to Bedfordshire the following January.

On my arrival at Woburn in early 1973 I was introduced to other residents of the oldest house in the village including Wally, my new roommate. He was an Irish labourer who muttered incoherently through a thick ginger beard. There was also much younger fellow who stayed there and worked as a kitchen assistant in the local Bedford Arms Hotel, he had his own room but had learning difficulties so conversation was limited, as it was also with the other elderly resident being in her nineties.

I started work on 5th January 1973 on another thick foggy morning. It was more than three weeks later before I saw any distant views of the park. Bedfordshire was a place of thick persistent fogs then.

On my first day of work I walked up the main road into

the park, past Drakeloe Lake then I turned left at Star Lodge by a cattle grid and up to buildings all dedicated to deer.

These had been constructed over a century ago and included a venison house for butchering deer with flagstones, bare wooden shelving and numerous rows of hooks and a hand winch.

Behind this was a large paddock made of wood and brick, a circular enclosure over 200 metres wide attached to more timber sheds designed for handling deer.

Deer hate corners. The paddocks and structures for containing deer were of solid boarded palisade to keep the deer quiet and were circular or had rounded corners. When placed in enclosures without corners there is less chance of injury.

Beyond the buildings were large paddocks surrounded by high metal railings over nine feet tall. They were home to small herds of deer including exotic Indian Axis and Rusa deer from Java.

On my first day of work I was greeted by Dennis (Mr Talbot) and Ian, who I was to work with and who would be my mentor and colleague and I was his new right-hand man.

In the adjacent round paddock I was soon introduced to a small black fallow buck yearling called Fellah and a Manchurian sika calf, both orphans, their mothers had had to be destroyed.

I soon learnt that Dennis had a back condition limiting what he was able to do physically, so he would be mainly our adviser, deer manager and marksman. He had been a professional cyclist before taking the Head Deer Keeper job which was quite a change of vocation but he knew a lot about the deer. He said he learnt much of it by listening to his predecessor who did most of the deer management from horseback.

My work mate Ian was a proud Scot and looked very much like the comedian Billy Connolly with his long dreadlocks and a goatie beard. He spoke with a strong Scottish accent which took me a while to understand. So, it was just the three of us to manage over 1200 deer and 3000 acres, the area over which the deer were able to roam freely.

My first job was to clean out the Land Rover. It was a truck cab so the rear part was covered by canvas. This was to become my mobile base and where although there were no seats, I would be spending most of the day bumping along in the back.

After loading the trailer with hay called the hay cart, Ian took me around the park in the Land Rover which was still immersed in fog but I was able to see some of the numerous deer herds as they emerged from the thick grey gloom. We cut the hay bales at the knot, so all the strings could be used again for other purposes, bundled up and taken back to the yard. Uncut bale strings can be fatal to deer if they get the loop caught on their antlers or around a leg, or both. An early lesson of good deer husbandry.

Woburn had a unique herd of Pere David deer that had become extinct in the wild, although there were about 350 adults in the park. These are not the most beautiful deer but nevertheless an important species of the deer world. They are rather ungainly with large bodied males weighing up to 230 kilos, and have long tails. Their eye and ears are small and they have long toes that click as they come together when walking. It is thought their long toes evolved because they lived in swampy ground somewhere in China.

It was ironic that we would be culling these animals despite their small numbers globally but it was not possible to move them alive anywhere else at the time. The other deer species I would be introduced to over the next few days were: Manchurian and Formosan Sika deer, Rusa from Java, Barasingha swamp deer from India and Axis or Chittal deer also from India, red and fallow, Chinese water deer and later I came across the secretive muntjac that lived mainly outside the park in the adjacent woodland.

The work at this time of year followed a regular routine; first was the feeding of all the well-scattered herds across the park and in paddocks, then catching and or culling followed later in the day.

Between January and early March we fed sugar beet and hay. The sugar beet was a large root crop each one weighing between two and four lbs, loaded by hand using pitchforks each morning into the back the Land Rover then taken around to the herds until the weather began improving and grass started to grow again.

I was informed by Ian, joking I thought, that from November to January we fed kale which we would be cutting by hand using a butchers cleaver! But it was true and did not sound fun, so that was something to really look forward to!

Having fed the deer and taking the hay cart, it felt very strange that to ensure the deer herds welfare we would pick up Mr Talbot with the rifle and then cull up to nine animals each day or sometimes more. We loaded the animals onto a trailer and took them back to the venison house where Ian taught me the Woburn way to gralloch (remove the stomach and vital organs) and how to skin the deer. I had already learnt the basics in gralloching techniques from Mike but this number of deer at any one time and their much greater sizes was on a more industrial scale compared to the smaller number I had encountered back in Gloucestershire, so I had to become proficient as well as work fast.

The skins as well as the carcass were valuable so they must not to be damaged or cut while skinning and this required another skill and an acquired technique, pushing the skin off the carcass and not using a knife. This was hard graft and would continue day after day through the winter months to achieve the cull targets. The quality of the final carcass was always important as game dealers and other clients were fussy and included customers in Germany, at Harrods, and the Abbey restaurant just up the road in the park.

After the hot sweaty work in the venison house we then had to stretch the ice cold deerskins across vertical wooden frames to air dry, which on a cold winters day is a finger numbing and character building task.

Considering I was paid £18 for a 42-hour week with no overtime, I reckon the estate had great value for money. Work was continuous, over seven days during winter, alternating our time at weekends to do the morning feed and herd check, before retiring home for a well-earned rest.

The summer was when the job became most satisfying. No

culling now unless we found an injury, so we spent time managing the permanent grassland, in spring chain harrowing, then spreading dried seaweed, an organic fertiliser, topping the grass to keep it palatable in parts of the park where the deer favoured grazing. We would clean out the wooden sheds in the paddocks, built specially for giving the deer some shelter.

Fences and gates were repaired and general estate maintenance done, which meant everything was in good condition before winter approached again.

During the summer months we spent time watching the herds with their new young, peacefully grazing in summer sunshine and if we came across calves and fawn lying in the grass, we would ear tag them, so we could keep records of their progress. We often met visitors in the park interested to know more about the animals.

I did get some holiday that year and it was my first visit to Scotland. I hitched from Newport Pagnell services with Ian all the way up to Crieff in Perthshire, where the annual Game Fair was being held that year. On the final stage of the journey north, late into the night I remember a large fully laden lorry of plywood stopping to take us both on board. The driver was keen to return to Hamilton, after driving up from London that same day. The noise in the lorry of the Atkins engine was deafening but in his rich Scottish accent he asked us to keep talking to him all the way to prevent him from falling asleep as he drove at high speed up and down the hills of the undulating road entering Scotland.

We were given numerous lifts in cars and lorries and after

19 hours we eventually reached our destination, walking the final few miles from Crieff town in blazing hot sunshine; weather I was not expecting.

We had made no accommodation plans for the visit so as the evening approached we decided to befriend a nearby farmer to ask if we could sleep overnight in his barn. He agreed and very generously also served up a fine meal that evening before we bedded down on the hay in his barn.

The following morning we made our way along the road to join the early queues to enter the Game fair which was a great day out. It was the showcase event for anyone involved and interested in hunting, shooting, fishing and the countryside with the local emphasis on the highlands.

There are various reasons why people choose to shoot. There are those who enjoy shooting for recreation and those who do it professionally as part of their job. There are also those who poach for the table and worst of all for commercial gain. Poachers are largely devoid of any respect or compassion for the animals, often causing serious injury and unnecessary suffering. We saw a mixture of all the above at the fair.

Although not an enjoyable task, selective culling is a key part of managing all deer. Relying on a finite source of food on diminishing land space and sometimes in an enclosed acreage, deer have no natural predator in Britain so a percentage of animals have to be removed annually, either by shooting for venison or by selling them alive. The culling at Woburn was done efficiently and humanely to maintain a mix of ages and sex ratios (stags to hinds) of the healthiest animals, so careful selection meant the weaker, oldest or late developers were taken out. The way a natural predator ideally selects its prey.

As we had a surplus of healthy animals as well, these would be the ones that were sold alive.

In my diary I kept a record of every animal that came through the venison house together with their weights etc. Some 374 animals were shot and then butchered by the two of us that year.

Diary excerpts:

January 10th 1973

Weather misty damp and cold.

Axis fawn found dead (still born) in sable paddock.

Manchurian sika buck age around 5-6 years darted using 8mm Susmolde colene. Deer dropped in 10 minutes and took 56 min to recover. It was in winter coat and had soiled underparts (late rut). Feet in good condition.

6 point head, short brows, thin beam, small coronet, body condition thin approx 160 lbs.

Tagged blue 13 Found to have worn teeth indicating an older animal.

6th February.

Dull sunny intervals 234 bales used.

8a.m. A muntjac fawn found half dead was dead 20 minutes later.

Darting. Vet Peter accompanying. Using Rompon to catch a Manchurian sika but was not successful try again tomorrow. Culling sika hind very thin 85 lbs dead weight.

Pere David knobbers have not yet cast all antler buds. Herd has split so only 40 at feed site.

29th January

Dull cold sunny intervals.

24 bales for Pere David herd. Axis buck still to cast other antler.

We tried to dart Manchurian sika although two darts hit they did not drop.

Beat up the Barasinga paddock for the estate keepers shoot to keep deer calm.

40 Pere David on the plains today.

7th Feb

Dull windy mild. 23 bales to P. David.

Catching using Immobilon. Vet in attendance 2 red stags 2 hinds and a calf darted successfully. Feeding done later.

24th October

Bright morning.

Took linseed to Sable paddock. Started feed circuit with Talbot. He culled 7 animals while doing the circuit included Manchuriian, 1 Fallow. I Legged (skinned) 6 of them in ¾ hour then hung the skins and finished feeding circuit. Formosan at Berry end, Swamp deer at Pekin paddock Talbot suggested we cut kale but we did not agree so did it the following morning!

To catch a deer

The part of work that I really enjoyed was the darting and catching of deer. The animals at Woburn had a fine pedigree and the deer that were in peak condition were purchased by other deer park owners to strengthen the health of their own herds. Such was the quality and bloodline of the Woburn Deer. The deer at Woburn were originally emparked by 11th Duke of Bedford in 1640 as part of a much larger animal menagerie and was thought to include lions and giraffe. The Woburn deer have commanded premium prices for live sales to stock new deer parks and deer herds around the world. We caught 173 live deer during my time at Woburn.

We had different techniques to catch the deer, these were; chasing with the Land Rover and catching by jumping off the vehicle onto an animal, catching smaller deer in nets found in release pens in the woodlands or by using a muscle relaxant tranquiliser with darts shot by compressed airguns.

We had to use the services of a vet to use the more potent drugs such as Immobilon and Rompun but we could use less lethal Susmold Colene independent of the vets.

Firing the dart into the right animal in exactly the right place was always the most difficult part because the dart is large and inaccurate, and for some reason the deer that you always want to catch seems to know you are after it, so it stays hidden behind its fellow herd members. Other deer stand in the way or look curiously at our circling around the herd in vehicles, seemingly fully aware that they are not the quarry that day.

The dart we used was small aluminium cylinder filled with a dose of drug and this is shot into the muscle of the animal by a special air rifle; as it hits the animal a blank .22 cartridge inside the dart is fired off and forces a plunger up the cylinder, forcing the drug into the animal.

The incredible muscular strength of the deer becomes apparent during these darting operations. The doses that were used could knock over much larger game animals but the deer always proved to be resistant to the drug because of a highly tuned metabolism reacting to stress.

It was imperative to reduce this stress on the animals once they lost power in their legs and lay on the ground, so great care was needed when approaching them. The first thing to do was to cover their eyes with a hessian cloth and then to work slowly and quietly. Such is their acute fear of man, when in close proximity with humans it can cause some deer to die of fright/stress. I am glad to say this was something we did not often experience, and it happened very rarely.

Occasionally after being revived from the drug, it can recycle through their system and this can be fatal.

With some younger animals we were even more cautious when darting them so we used even lower doses of tranquiliser. The animals were only partly sedated and had to be restricted from kicking out using leather straps to bind their legs when moving them from a tarpaulin to the final destination in the back of the Land Rover!

When the antidote called Revivon had been given to the animal it would be up on its feet almost immediately. On two occasions red stags destined for other parts of the world actually broke out of the wooden crates before they left the park. These were not pursued again but were allowed to stay, having shown their spirit to remain at Woburn.

Being a deer keeper was a pretty tough and physical job and it also took its toll on my clothing. The bloodstained and rotted material and my jeans were often ripped during catching operations. I have always been interested in leather and the wide range of uses it can be put to, so I decided to purchase two kip skins, or calf hides, from a tannery that we used in Leighton Buzzard. Cutting them to shape of my legs with my German Puma skinning knife and using leather bootlace thong I laced the two sides together to make a pair of chaps. A few belt loops added with some rough stitching to keep them up and they slid over my jeans to give full protection from my work duties. Little did I know then that by making these chaps would be the first of many more leather projects in future years. Ian soon asked for a pair and for a belt too.

Woburn is an enormous park covering 3000 acres so we would spend many hours patrolling the park and checking the 12-mile perimeter wall for breaches and to make sure any injured or weak deer that had left their herds were attended to and not left to a lingering death.

This original landscape is an ancient one of early 17th century grazed by herds of large herbivores. The park comprises of permanent grassland, artificial lakes and many scattered 300-400 year old oak and hawthorn trees. This was a landscape influenced by early landscape gardeners including Repton and was later recreated on many other estates by Capability Brown described as picturesque parkland. Our ancient forests that were once protected for game would have looked similar, a habitat described as wood pasture. These were multifunctional spaces where trees were grown for timber and firewood, while game and other livestock grazed beneath the trees.

This landscape at Woburn is typical of a deer park, much of it undulating wooded grassland offering warm sheltered banks of bracken where the deer spend time escaping the flies and giving birth on the quiet undisturbed slopes. Many of the oak trees have wide spreading branches sometimes reaching down to the ground. At the time I did not fully appreciated just how special and important these trees and parklands habitats are.

Wood pasture has become increasingly rare, lost under the plough, buildings and roads. Yet these places are rich with life and biodiversity and thrives in and around ancient trees and unimproved grassland, in the protected soils beneath them that have never been ploughed or affected by chemical fertilisers.

We often saw other wildlife on our patrols when we would shoot some of the numerous rabbits that inhabited the park and were a welcome tasty meal. One morning we came across a stoat sitting on top of what we thought was a dead rabbit as it was not moving and the stoat was chewing into the back of its neck.

Ian decided he fancied this rabbit for supper so, as he stealthily approached the two animals, the stoat saw him coming and it quickly ran off, followed to our great surprise and just as quickly, by the rabbit! It must have been in some kind of trance. It is thought that the weasel family, mustelids, which include stoats, are able to mesmerise their prey including rabbit until it is killed. On this occasion Ian lost his rabbit as did the stoat, who had not ventured far away but stayed watching bemused by our interest from behind the buttress root of a nearby oak tree.

On another occasion one September afternoon we came across a red deer hind looking distressed and on closer inspection found that she had a crossbow bolt embedded in her eye. She had a calf with her. This confirmed our suspicions that we always had that poachers were operating in the park at night using crossbows and dogs.

We reluctantly had to shoot both the mother and the calf because it was too big and wild to take in under our wing. It was at times like this that made me quite ashamed of humans and despised their callous action causing suffering and the unnecessary slaughter of two perfectly healthy animals.

Other untold and unseen horrors were no doubt regularly committed in the park which we sadly had no way of stopping but relied on police and others to keep their eyes peeled. One night some lads were stopped by police and found a deer carcass in their car but had no weapon so were free to go. Both the weapon and the carcass must be found together for a potential prosecution.

Poaching is a heinous activity pursued by ruthless people with no respect for animals, unconcerned about the pain and suffering they cause. While this may sound odd coming from someone involved in the frequent death of so many deer, the big difference is that each deer we removed is carefully selected, then humanely shot by a professional marksman who had a high regard and respect for the animals and never left any to die a slow lingering death, which many poachers seem quite happy to do.

During my time at Woburn we found 152 dead deer around the park that year, which sounds an awful lot but many were breach or dead calves and fawns while a number of them were also road casualties, a public road cut through the park, but I am sure a good percentage of the remainder were the victims of poaching, as we often found marks on the animals that would indicate injuries from dogs. These deer would have died slowly from their injuries and from shock.

Although attempts were often made to try and count exactly how many deer there were in the park, it was always a very difficult task to achieve accurate numbers. The local deer society spent a day with us but I do not think we counted the number that we thought were actually there.

It is an even more difficult task to count deer in the wider landscape. As a rule of thumb we always thought that for every deer you actually see there is another, or perhaps two that you don't see.

Although it was physically challenging, I was enjoying most of the work at Woburn but I was becoming increasingly fed up with the digs that I had to share with Wally and the others. The company was not ideal for a young lad, food was frankly pretty average and Wally liked his Guinness with orange drink, which meant lots of grunting and snoring, all rather unsociable when trying to get a good night sleep!

In May, I eventually plucked up courage to ask the estate if I could rent one of many cottages that were around the estate. I was not married, which meant I did not qualify but reluctantly they agreed and I was offered a small cottage. I took up residence in Husborne Crawley in a two bedroom cottage and was opposite one of the lodge entrances to the park. Barry and Carol were my neighbours who were very friendly Londoners and were great entertainment. Barry worked as builder on the estate.

The cottage needed decorating so I painted it with a mix of orange and purple which, looking back now seems a rather odd choice, but that seemed fashionable at the time.

Having private space also allowed me to enjoy my music in peace at last.

My new walk to work was a commute to remember. It was about a mile and went through the Evergreens, a large mature coniferous woodland with many rhododendrons, around a large part of the park perimeter. The route took me through a dark green forest and along a narrow road behind the safari park fence where exotic noises were often heard. Anything from lions roaring to whistling dolphins contrasted with guttural belches of the Bactrian camels all filling the air under a canopy of very English oak trees, before reaching the deer HQ.

The dolphins arrived the year while I was working at Woburn and I was introduced to them and given some special moments in the new purpose-built building with a large pool.

The Evergreens was well populated with muntjac deer, a small deer introduced from China by a previous Duke. Just 18 inches high with small antlers and sharp tusks, a hangover from their prehistoric sabre toothed evolution. We lured some of these muntjac into the pheasant release pens, when not in use for pheasant rearing, before catching them in a long net. They were sold to wildlife parks and private collections. In hindsight this was not a wise practice!

It was while doing this catching that I suffered my first real injury from an animal. I was cut by one of the sharp tusks of an angry buck. Its sharp tusk cut through my index finger so I went on the bus to Bedford hospital to be given just one stitch. I then bought the *Sabbath Bloody Sabbath* album which seemed appropriate after all the bloodshed!

Muntjac would lie quietly under the rhododendron bushes before rushing off as soon as you made eye contact. They always seem to know when you have seen them and would scurry off at speed with a bark, head down and a raised white tail. Muntjac are also called barking deer due to their rasping bark when disturbed or frightened.

These deer as well as rhododendron, grey squirrels, knotweed and Himalayan balsam, are all introduced species that have become serious threats to our native plants and animals. They have become major threat to our landscape having all successfully been introduced by collectors and Victorians and have spread across Great Britain over the last 150 years, displacing our native flora and fauna. If not controlled effectively given the increasing numbers and distribution of these species, we may lose many native woodland plants including the iconic bluebell and some orchids. This is a lesson we must learn from, at a time of increasing global movements of plants, soils and timber from far flung countries. Diseases are even arriving in packing cases and on flotsam floating in across the Atlantic helping to give exotic species a lift to reach our shores.

The sad fact is that most of the invasive species have been left alone for years to breed and spread. This is a result of not having joined up policies or well informed professional wildlife management resources in the UK.

High numbers of deer together with the introduced grey squirrel are a continuing threat to our woodland and treescape and the damage these animals cause should not to be underestimated.

We need to take a pragmatic and professional approach to seeking the eradication of these plants, the grey squirrel and if possible muntjac deer. Their removal over time should be a clear objective for landowners as well as to manage sustainable numbers of fallow, sika, roe and red deer and now wild boar.

Our native deer on the other hand can, in the right numbers, play an important part in maintaining woodland diversity by ecologically engineering our countryside. Woodland pasture is a rich habitat where deer have played a pivotal role over centuries to establish and maintain such places.

Today more animals including deer and boar are being seen increasingly on roadside verges and in gardens which may indicate a shortage of feeding/forage ground in the adjacent conifer forests and across the wider farmed countryside.

I Meet Some Elephants

To help pay the cottage rent I offered to share it with Stephen, a chap I had met briefly when he stayed with Mrs Goodwin as another lodger when he first started work in the elephant section of the adjacent Safari park. He soon moved to a caravan but found it too cold and damp.

Our friendship gave me the opportunity to help Stephen at weekends with the five young elephants that he was partly responsible for. I offered to work there in my spare time at weekends, helping to feed and then oversee them while out in the picnic area.

In the mornings and before the park was open to the public, after giving the elephants a hearty breakfast, this was enough food to fill the back of a trailer, we would take them along a mile walk through the rhino section and up to the picnic area where the public could view them behind a strand of electric fence wire.

Having such close contact with these animals was a privilege and they made me feel very humble and acutely aware of just how intelligent they are.

Examples of this would be – if they did not want one of their night shackles released in the morning, they would simply lean away from you putting the release bolt under strain and making it impossible to turn it. They would look down at you with a knowing look showing a white part of their eye, as if to say, just wait and we'll do this in my own time mate!

After a few minutes they would relax, allowing the shackle to be released.

Another time, while in the picnic area, there was a lot of ear flapping going on, which indicates the elephants are agitated or are looking for mischief, so when one of them came up to be friendly, intent on distracting me by carefully shielding my sight from one of its fellow troop, which then proceeded to put its foot carefully on one of the electric fence posts around the temporary enclosure and push it flat on the ground, before walking over it to give chase to an un unsuspecting pheasant. The silly bird had been strutting about outside the enclosure fence and the elephants obviously considered it as a good bit of sport by chasing it. Such was the elephants endearing sense of play and ability to conspire and work together.

To think these animals could easily disappear forever in the wild is quite intolerable and unacceptable and question whether we humans should have the privilege to inhabit this planet.

Other experiences at Woburn

As I had little money and the locals in the pubs were persistent in asking for free venison or antlers, I spent the dark evenings after work at the very grand Woburn Abbey Sculpture gallery restaurant. This is where I helped out as a wine waiter late into the night serving wine to wealthy guests including Americans who came to enjoy the fine food. Quite a contrasting role from my day job! They flew over by jet to Heathrow and travelled by coach up the M1 to the abbey for a banquet before returning to America.

Returning to the deer park, Ian my work mate was a great character and we worked well together. I was not quite 18 but he soon allowed me to drive the Land Rover off-road, as I had no driving license at the time but I had driven tractors in the past.

What better way to learn to drive than in a large private park on quiet roads and over rough terrain and to be able to experience driving in all weather conditions? Ian told me to get the vehicle stuck on purpose so that I learnt how to recover it again and to know how to avoid putting the vehicle into unwise places in the first place. I also learnt to manoeuvre trailers into narrow gateways, into barn entrances and along deeply rutted tracks. It got very exciting when I was trusted to drive during some darting operations and had to cover the ground at speed to keep up with the animals after they had been darted. This was another skill learnt as a deer keeper which would prove to be very useful in future years.

Ian also shared my great interest in music and he introduced me to Pink Floyd and Genesis. I was already a fan of Black Sabbath, Deep Purple and Santana which seemed a paradox that I also loved the peace and quiet of the countryside while embracing very noisy rock bands. I was also a keen self-taught drummer, although my music teacher told me I could not pitch notes so should leave music alone; which I did and never had a chance to be taught at school to play them.

The winter routine

Although naively I thought cutting the kale by hand was a joke made on my arrival in January, it was true and was something I had to look forward to in the approaching early winter months. Kale is like a tall Brussels sprout and thrives in cold wet places. When frosty it is covered in ice and water, which sprays you as you cut the woody stem. After cutting five rows, 30 metres long each morning we would be pretty cold and wet, just like the kale, so we warmed up in the Land Rover with perhaps a drop of whisky in the flask of tea or we used the heat from the exhaust pipe to bring feeling back into our fingers.

Bending over to do this work also gave you backache pretty quickly, not helped by the freezing wind that blew up your backside. It was a ritual done every morning and lasting for about an hour and really separated the men from the boys! Strangely enough we did not get any volunteers offering to help!

After loading the kale onto the trailer it was a short trip back into the deer park, driving past the safari park to distribute the kale to the various scattered herds.

Using the pitch fork like a tuning fork ringing against the metal trailer brought hundreds of galloping deer out of the thick mist and up to the trailer to claim a stem of kale. This was a sight never to be forgotten and it soon took your mind off the aching back from kale cutting. The clicking sound of the hundreds of long toes was particularly striking as they gathered alongside the trailer.

Having fed the kale the routine was to load up another hay cart, usually about 25 bales, to keep the deer in good spirits during the wet and cold weather. While Ian or Mr Talbot drove and were sitting comfortably in the warm, I was stationed on the top of the bales, lurching from side to side, as we drove slowly around the park, along the slopes and shallow valleys where the deer congregated and I scattered slabs of hay in a line behind the trailer, keeping each slab spaced far enough apart to prevent animals injuring others with their antlers.

After the hay cart a quick arming-up session with the rifle was usually needed, before we would set off for more culling or catching for the rest of the day, if there was enough time and the weather was suitable!

Just over 14 months at Woburn and after months of culling I suppose I was homesick and rather depressed and had had enough of the amount of shooting, blood and gore involved.

I felt I had acquired some very special experience and

learnt a lot about deer and their management. Such was the scale of the operation at Woburn that I thought 12 months there had to equate to five years at least in any other deer park. The Bedford clay gave me bad vibes as well so it was not a place for me to stay long term. I decided to leave and return to Bristol. Mike my friend back in Gloucestershire was talking about a possible job opportunity becoming available with the deer there, so optimistically I said farewell to Dennis and Ian and returned to Bristol.

What I Learnt

After leaving school I remember being averse to any killing of animals or to any bloodshed, so the shooting of the black buck in Bristol was a sobering and enlightening moment for me. I would not have gone to Woburn without that experience. That day I came to understand even more clearly that we had to respect wild animals and consider very carefully the impact we have on their welfare and wellbeing so that we can continue to live in harmony with them in a crowded world. Animals and landscapes have to be managed together, they are inseparable. Having lost the natural predators of deer in Britain it now requires man to become the apex predator when necessary. Ironically, killing an animal for humane reasons, to stop suffering or to remove a threat to other fellow animals can be in the best long term interest of the species survival. This is a fact of life that we all need to understand better. The Pere David deer at Woburn may well have become extinct years ago if the few remaining animals had not been taken to Woburn and the thriving new herd conserved by culling.

We should also value the native wild deer resource living wild in our countryside and appreciate better that they need to be managed professionally.

Deer are wild and very powerful animals, they have highly developed senses, so to shoot or catch a deer requires respect and knowledge of the animal, great patience and skill.

Deer can read your mind! Never shout or move quickly in the presence of deer.

Before shooting any deer leave the gun at home until you know your deer well and you understand what you are seeing and know which ones are the right ones to cull.

To get to know them well, observation is the key. The animals will usually tell you if it is ill or has a problem. An angular body and arched back means it is in poor condition. Being on its own often means it could be sick or perhaps about to have a calf/fawn.

Early moulting in spring however often means an animal is in good condition.

If disturbed a calf fawn will run in a circle to return back to its "couch" where its mother placed it. They also often return to their place of birth later in their life.

Dogs and the public should keep well away from deer and to leave them alone and in peace. The dog might want to play but deer do not.

Deer always know when you have seen them, some kind of sixth sense kicks in. They also seem to know which species of deer you are about catch or cull that day.

They will always prove you wrong. Never underestimate what they are capable of.

Deer hate wet and cold conditions combined, just like us.

Catching and translocation is expensive so moving live animals around should be carefully considered. If allowed to escape they can potentially spread diseases or establish non-native species into the landscape as has happened with Sika and muntjac.

When male deer become weakened from too much rutting or suffer from a wound they will deteriorate quickly and spend time away from the herd. They can however survive major injuries, mend broken limbs and ribs if in otherwise good condition at the time.

They often go to water and immerse themselves when distressed or are under threat.

Although free of most disease in the wild, deer can contract tuberculosis, blue tongue and Enzootic ataxia, this is a condition affecting nerves and their balance, caused probably by a copper deficiency. They can survive foot and mouth disease.

Frequent observation and monitoring deer is vital to know what is happening on your land, to understand the deer habits and their movements.

Having a patient quiet manner is key attribute of working with deer (and other wild animals) and the ability to think like a deer is something that can only be learnt slowly and over time.

Despite the best intentions by some well-meaning organisations, animal suffering can be prolonged by trying to administer first aid and applying principles better suited to domestic animals. First aid can prolong stress and can play a part in why many wild animals eventually just keel over and die in captivity.

It is far more humane to make an early despatch within 12 hours when an animal is seriously injured and its condition is in decline. Some animals left in their natural environment can however survive major injuries in the wild if they are not subjected to stress and there is no threat from a natural predator. Careful judgement is required to know the best action to take.

Road collisions with deer are increasing each year and cause suffering to the animals as well as human injury and even some fatalities. To help reduce the threat trees and shrubs should be cut back from roads and of course drivers should slow down.

Fences erected through woodland and across deer tracks with wire strands attached along the top of the fence line can become a lethal trap for the deer's legs as they leap over the fence, often trapping a foot and causing a long slow lingering death.

To control deer you must put all your wits against the animal to stalk them, it requires patience and knowledge of the deer behaviour and be able to second guess the animals' movements.

To always be aware that the bullets you are using can travel up to a mile and beyond.

Stalking a weak or injured deer to achieve a quick death by a well-aimed shot, can be a most satisfying feeling of a job well done.

Poaching causes immense suffering.

Shooting female deer is the most effective way of reducing deer populations, not by trophy hunting for males.

Seeking excitement by shooting a deer is never in the best interest of the animal. It should be conducted calmly, professionally and pragmatically for the overall best long term interest of the deer population. This approach will ensure deer and the herds remain healthy and that the fittest animals breed in future.

For some people shooting deer raises adrenal levels, so much so that they can become delirious and almost paralysed after shooting an animal, this is called buck fever.

We must not overlook the fact that we have intervened for centuries to manipulate and change the ecology of the landscape in the UK, not always wisely, but we cannot turn our backs on it now thinking it will all be just fine if we leave everything alone.

This is why we need to be better at managing wildlife and the landscape in which we all live together with an expanding human population.

We have important choices and decisions to make based on our knowledge and learning from history, not just by pure science, because science does not know all the answers yet. We need to try things out based on experience and continue the traditions that we know work best.

We also need to listen and learn from the wisdom of people who have knowledge and practical experience and not from politicians, developers, accountants and managers.

Venison is also one of the most delicious meats you will ever eat and the liver is sublime.

CHAPTER 9

MY NEXT ADVENTURE
IN BRISTOL

Back in Bristol, unfortunately the job Mike mentioned with deer did not actually materialise as I had hoped. Living at home in Hallen again and after a few unproductive weeks being unemployed, I signed on at an temporary employment agency offering various jobs which soon convinced me that I had to get back to the wild again.

The first place I worked was for an engineering firm, then I joined an architects' practice operating a printing machine and even a spent few weeks at Rolls Royce listing all the component parts for Concorde onto a computer. This reminded me of the encouragement from my career master years ago to work there. I am very glad I did not listen to him. After a few weeks at each location I soon left all the jobs.

This urban life seemed very strange and alien to me and the pubs and nightclubs where my temporary new colleagues congregated were not my scene at all, I found them hot, claustrophobic and threatening places. However, while in *civilisation* it was an opportunity to pass my driving test.

I acquired my license at the first attempt, helped I am sure by my driving experience at Woburn. I was now mobile and able to use my mother's Ford Anglia and make weekend visits to the old deer park cottage where I continued to help Mike with the occasional culling while also enjoying brief spells of real country life again.

Later in 1974 I was able to leave the city noise by using my previous cross country course building experience. I had been recommended to the owners of a newly established equitation centre and combined cookery school. Ronald, one of the owners, asked me to build some fences for schooling horse and riders. I happily took on the challenge and was presented with an old blue Fordson tractor, a chainsaw, some second-hand telegraph poles and railway sleepers and left to get on with it.

I constructed some good solid fences which were well received by the pupils, mostly girls. I enjoyed their company and sampled their delicious food that was produced each lunch time so I developed a taste for fine food. I inevitably got to know one of the pupils well, she was called Hilary and we spent an all too brief but memorable time together. Wishbone Ash and Santana's *Abraxas* was the music we both enjoyed listening to during those warm summer evenings.

Sadly things had to change as the students finished their courses, I had built all the fences and we went our separate ways.

Back to the wild and learning how to survive and respect the planet

That winter I reluctantly returned to find some work in Bristol again and found myself working in the Display and Promotions section of a large department store in the centre of Bristol. I cannot actually remember how or why I got the job but it was a great fun surprisingly, immersed in a fast-moving retail world with a good team of very different creative people. I remember making all manner of display props and signage and even cutting out large Wombles for the Christmas grotto from a material called Essex board. I spent time up ladders hanging signs and moving manikins around in large window displays as passing shoppers looked on curiously.

Going from the rusticity of the riding school and deer park to the hot lights of a busy department store was to experience two very contrasting worlds.

After about seven months I eventually felt I really needed to move on from the display job, increasingly concerned that my original career aspirations were looking very distant. I was writing for other jobs all over the place but I could find very few opportunities and no guidance was available.

Having continued helping out at weekends in the deer park, Mike suggested I could stay in the cottage there in return for maintaining it in good condition and to help look after King his dog, a mad German pointer (Mike's wife expelled King from their home due to his crazy behaviour). The offer of the cottage was quickly accepted and I was given use of Mike's Land Rover, on which I later painted a stag's head, as well as having the use of his mini clubman at weekends when Mike would visit from time to time over that coming summer.

With no other work in prospect that summer, one the hottest, I returned to the nearby riding school to build and replace more fences. These were halcyon and very memorable days.

The riding school had grown and become a successful bustling place with aspiring equestrians with their horses, learning dressage, show jumping, leaping over my cross country fences and cooking. So I continued again to enjoy delicious lunchtime meals produced in the old farmhouse kitchen by the cordon bleu students.

The owner was now a qualified farrier who spent most of his time cursing the horses as they recoiled from his attempts to re-shoe them. He had a neighbour called William, a young gentleman "farmer" who, although I did not know at the time, would later become a very good friend and a major influence over my future.

During 1975 I lived in the cottage for over six months. It had no running water so I had to pump up it from a deep well outside with a hand pump, there was no electricity or central heating but a large inglenook fireplace. It was at the far end of the deer park, a long way from the nearest road offering a way of life that I think all of us should experience, at least for a little while.

Living simply in such an isolated environment is surely the best way to learn how much effort is actually needed to just survive and be able to sustain a basic but good quality of life.

We should never take the basics of life for granted and we need to better appreciate where our food and materials come from. It is so important to remember how to grow food and useful materials from a healthy soil and from the wider countryside, not just from farmland, but also from shrubs, trees and from our woodlands.

By living this way, simply and close to nature, you learn to understand how everything in nature is connected and you become very aware of the seasons and the changes around you, of the climate, the trees, animals and the plants. Living in Park Wall cottage put me back in touch with my natural surroundings again, which so few of us are able to do today.

The surrounding countryside around Park Wall cottage was idyllic. Not only were the usual birds always seen and heard but also nightingales sang there through the night; this was the only place in England that I had heard their beautiful song. Badger cubs wandered from their sett before dusk, impatient to wait for darkness, while the wild deer materialised out of the woodland into the field outside the cottage and disappeared just as quickly. Buzzards were always soaring over the park calling their plaintiff mewing cry.

After returning from my regular evening forays listening and watching all this life around me I would spend the nights listening to little known album tracks on Radio Caroline as the tawny owls hooted outside in the trees. Caroline was the only station that played my type of music; Wishbone Ash, Mike Oldfield, Pink Floyd – and in stark contrast I also enjoyed John Denver.

It was in this rare and isolated environment away from modern twentieth century that I continued to make various leather items and began practicing carving leather. This was a new craft I had taken up while living at home.

Ever since I had made the leather chaps at Woburn some years ago I was still being asked to make belts, bags and even a gun case. I was now carving animal designs onto leather. Although I had a good set of tools, my leather craft skills still had some room for improvement.

Living in this remote cottage and driving a Land Rover attracted attention and a little curiosity from some of the riding school residents as I toiled away building cross country fences in the fields. At lunch times while enjoying the latest culinary delights of their cooking it was a perfect opportunity to get to know the students, while not on their horses. I got to know two girls at the same time, both of whom I became great friends with.

I fell for Diana first, she was from Dorset. We had a great time visiting the local pubs, introducing her to the wildlife that she shared my love of. Her great friend was Frances, she was a tall elegant girl from Buckinghamshire who I also fell head over heels for and rather guiltily, I spurned Diana to court Frances, although we all still stayed friends somehow.

Warm summer evenings with Frances were spent walking and visiting more local pubs, enjoying each other's company and spending time in the deer park, sitting under the great oaks then later in front of the log fire in the cosy cottage as the pink sun dipped below the horizon. At the end of the summer Frances and Diana finished their courses and they moved on. I continued to build the fences but it was very different now.

All good things come to an end and I had to find some long term work again. I was still getting letters from Diana who had taken employment as a groom in a large house in the Chilterns and Frances was also there working with her.

Although I had no car of my own and very little money, hitching a lift was how I travelled about. I decided to visit them both, it was new part of the country that I did not know and I eventually reached Stokenchurch, after walking through endless beech woodland, I finally found the large house where the girls were living and working, overlooking a beautiful valley near Fingest.

Although a complete stranger I was kindly entertained by the owner of the house until the girls returned from their ride. Surprised to see me Diana was friendly but Frances was preoccupied most of the time with a new boyfriend on the phone, so we did not have a lot to say. After enjoying their company and a drink in the nearby Fox Inn I spent the night sleeping in a barn just below the house, before walking ten miles back to High Wycombe.

As fate has it, and in some desperation I finished up getting a job as a postman in the town and on the same day managed to find some digs that were owned by a cockney landlord who was the double of Ronnie Barker's four candle/fork handle character. I had to convince him I was an honourable man as I had little money to pay the rent, until I was paid my first wage from the Post office.

I stayed in Wycombe doing the postman job for six months,

driving to outlying villages and walking up and down the numerous steps around the Wycombe houses, each with countless steps delivering the mail.

I bought my first car there, a blue Triumph Herald. Although a beautiful piece of countryside, the Chilterns was not where I wanted to continue doing what I was doing and knew I needed to move back to wildlife.

CHAPTER 10

BADGERS NEED HELP

It was while working in High Wycombe sorting office that I noticed a copy of a *Farmers Weekly* magazine with damaged packaging left on a table. It had an article about bovine tuberculosis (bTB) and the work of MAFF as it was called then, today we know it as DEFRA. The article stated that it was about to embark on an experimental TB control programme with badgers that were believed by the vets, to pass the disease on to cattle. They were looking people to join teams who would be working in Gloucestershire and some other counties around the south west.

My career path had well and truly lost its way at this point so this looked interesting.

Always having a soft spot for badgers and spending many hours in the woods watching them, I also took two of them around in a minivan to the WIs with David Chaffe while working at the wildlife park, I was sure I could use all this experience and be a useful member of the team! I also thought that I could, just perhaps, have some influence into how this unsavoury work was to actually be executed, literally. I immediately wrote off for an application form and was duly invited along to an interview.

I drove to Chipping Sodbury and was interviewed by a large imposing panel of people and I was offered one of the jobs available. With this welcome news I was able to say goodbye to the Royal Mail and return to Bristol again.

In February 1976 I started working as a *process supervisor* or better described as a field officer. The job was based in Thornbury which was not far to travel from home, so Mother had to put up with me living at home again.

Working for MAFF

The work we were to do included liaison with farmers and landowners, walking miles of countryside surveying farms for badger setts, and gassing operations, which I was not looking forward to. I had some previous experience of the survey work already, but I had not done any of the wretched gassing.

As the work teams were assembled I found myself working with people of very mixed backgrounds and experience, from local keeper/poacher, to a farmer, an ex-builder and a few even more colourful characters shall we say! Initially we spent days walking the fields and woods looking for the badger setts. We would then carry out gassing operations, but we very soon began to doubt its effectiveness as setts had to be gassed and gassed again, calling into question the method and effectiveness of such operations. As the gassing progressed more badger tracks were being increasingly observed, emerging from previously gassed setts, so it was obviously not working.

It was difficult for me to come to terms with this aspect of the work and I am very glad that our concerns were taken seriously it was eventually outlawed.

Ernest Neal had written a fine book about badgers but so little was actually known about their ecology or behaviour. We knew hardly anything about the structure of a sett or about the bTB disease itself, or why the badger in particular seemed to be vulnerable to this disease.

The badger had consequently become considered by some to be a pest, like a rabbit or a rat. We had to learn much more about this persecuted animal and I now had an opportunity to help.

We were working for the Pest Infestation Control Laboratory (PICL) based at Worplesdon, Surrey, the research arm into animal ecology and animal health, so I became involved in a range of different and interesting tasks that were not unfamiliar to me.

These included live trapping of small mammals for testing for bTB, these mostly came back negative. Also surveying for signs of badger activity including tracks and dung pits to begin to learn about territory sizes around badger setts.

Then we needed to understand the effect of pumping a gas into a badger sett. To do this we methodically excavated and professionally surveyed two "surface setts" by hand. This had not been done before and we learnt a lot about the layout of the setts that are dug by badgers over generations.

Two setts were excavated by hand, each had tunnels extending a total length of over a quarter of a mile. The setts were then reconstructed in order to conduct mock gassing trials using a dye and numerous sampling points which confirmed that gas was not reaching the whole sett.

It later transpired by trials done at Porton Down that badgers were suffering by being gassed with cyanide and thankfully, at last, the use of gas came to an end and was banned.

Later in 1976 we also began to work with another research section of PICL in the Cotswolds at a private park in a secluded valley being used as a research site to learn more about badger ecology. Over the next few years we surveyed every square foot of the 600 acre densely wooded valley called Woodchester. Every sett and dung pit was recorded and gradually much more of our time was spent doing ecological monitoring and surveys.

My diary in May 1977 records the hours that I worked one night;

Start 10:00 p.m. finish 1:45 a.m. home by 2:45 a.m and records the following account:

I was clinging onto the bonnet of a Land Rover late at night being driven across fields to catch Reg, a radio collared badger and I used a large landing net to catch him. I pounced onto the animal covering it with the net, we used a drug Vetalin to tranquilise it, so we could handle it safely and take samples of blood, nasal discharge and sputum, and check condition before releasing him back to the beech tree sett. This was the same sett featured on television on 9th May when Phil Drabble was the presenter and BBC filmed the sett in the early days of live broadcasting using remote cameras, well before the days of *Autumn Watch*.

We also did a lot bait marking over subsequent years as well as radio telemetry work, live cage trapping, tattooing, blood sampling and weighing, etc. We perfected the live cage trapping technique of using green garden twine instead of heavy metal pedals to spring the live cage trap.

The bait marking operations involved feeding badgers with peanuts, honey/syrup mixed with a range of coloured plastic pellets. Each sett was fed with a different colour. After consuming the peanut bait their dung was used by the badger to mark its presence in some of the many latrine pits around its territory, leaving a calling card with a few coloured pellets showing which sett it had come from and confirming the extent of each territory. It also confirmed that most of these animals largely stayed within their own area year on year.

In my diary it records that in June 1978 we caught over 100 badgers and tagged 78 over just a few weeks after using this new technique and that we had caught more badgers than at any previous time.

This was really interesting work and much was being learnt about badger ecology, the size of each sett territory, how and where they spent time every night, how far they travelled and what relationships they had with other badgers and with cattle. We learnt how badgers were always marking their territory and that most of the badgers stayed within it, only boars making excursions to other setts.

The work included live capture of numerous badgers, marking them and recording the details of each one, so we acquired a full life history of the many social groups living in the valley.

Occasionally we caught animals that were obviously sick. They were scarred and often underweight, thin hair covering their bodies, their ears torn indicating numerous fights. The more these animals wandered into adjacent territories the more fights they found themselves in and this probably also had potential to increase the risk of spreading any disease from one animal to another.

Although we hold these animals with great affection, badgers have a tough life and can be very aggressive to other badgers. They have powerful jaws and sharp teeth which need to be carefully avoided when handling them, even under sedation.

While tracking these animals we found out that some badgers frequented the same few fields and sometimes farm buildings which could greatly increase any potential risk of spreading a disease by cross contamination onto cattle food. These barns were often open fronted and easy for badgers and other animals to enter.

The work into bTB cattle and badgers has continued to this day, 40 years later, so I am bewildered and disappointed when I see news items about badger research being done that is seemingly repeating this work again and ignoring what has already been found out about badgers and understanding more about bTB and cattle. A great amount was learned through doing this work which sadly seems to have been largely disregarded and that crude shooting (not culling) has been introduced, probably to appease some farming interest wanting to see badger numbers reduced. Killing them regardless of the badger's age or condition is overlooking the bigger picture and the impact that modern farming and modern development is having on habitats and all wild animal populations including the badger.

It is still far from proven that badgers are the only threat to cattle, given that a small percentage are found with the TB disease at an advanced or infectious stage.

Instead I think we need to concentrate more on the cattle, how they are bred and managed, to improve the herd biosecurity and change land management practices. I would suggest that it is vital to maintain adequate permanent foraging areas for wild animals and to reduce cattle movements. It is also thought by some well-informed people that the badgers could develop an immunity to diseases including bTB over seven generations. This cannot happen if we continue shooting badgers including the healthy ones!

It also seems strange to me that an animal suffering from a supposedly fatal disease continues to maintain its numbers. This despite the culling and not forgetting the high number of road kills by vehicle numbers as well. It does not add up.

The earthworm is the main diet of badgers so good healthy meadows/grassland and its soil is where the worms are most numerous and is where the badgers spend their nights foraging. Artificial fertiliser and annual ploughing destroys worms so it is not surprising the badger now has less food available today than in the past.

The more we remove these natural forage areas then the more pressure will be put on the animals to use other places to find food. This is another good reason for allowing field margins and areas of unimproved grassland to thrive on all farms.

Using organic fertiliser not only improves the soil structure it also replaces the need for chemical fertilisers that kill organisms in the soil

It may also be worth considering using the new solar farms being widely established to provide valuable additional forage areas on land that are not intensively farmed.

What I have learnt

Badgers are very territorial, most stay within their territories for most of their lives. There is a high natural mortality rate exacerbated by road collisions.

They adapt their diet through the year but rely heavily on good soil with earthworms. They do not usually interface closely with cattle in fields.

They prefer permanent longer grass and scrubby areas to forage in and have a very mixed diet, similar to a pig. Increasing the amount of decaying wood could enhance the range of food available.

Badgers will sometimes use farm building to find food. Sick animals in particular will become solitary and can be found foraging during the daylight hours.

Badgers are difficult to trap. Even more difficult to shoot humanely near to setts.

Left undisturbed and with enough foraging space they are more likely to happily remain within their territorial limits marked by dung pits year on year and inter-generationally.

bTB can survive ultra-violet (UV) sunlight and remain in an infectious state on the ground for days. It can therefore be passed to other animals such as deer, not just badgers.

Giving more space on farms for badgers to forage could reduce the incidence of bTB cross contamination to cattle which is still yet to be proven beyond all doubt.

Vaccination of badgers has proved to work and is cheaper than culling. It is hoped a vaccination for cattle can be produced in time.

In order to control bTB all infected cattle must be removed from the national herd. At the moment Defra is failing to do this. Defra have themselves confirmed the skin test is routinely missing many infected cattle. This leads to a high probability of residual herd infection contributing to the recurrence of the disease in high risk areas and to other parts of the country. Considering the 14 million cattle movement in the UK this is a factor currently being overlooked by Defra. If this is not addressed there is little if any chance of seeing the bTB being controlled.

This undiagnosed reservoir of infection poses the greatest challenge in the reduction of bTB that government departments and the NFU need to address.

Hallen and changes to local area

A pony and trap outing along the lanes with the family.

Sitting on the hollow log in 10 acre field.

A view of my home in 1975.

Similar view in 2000 showing the development all around.

The M5 motorway going south, east of the village.

The M5 slicing its path through Berwick woodland.

Map and aerial photo

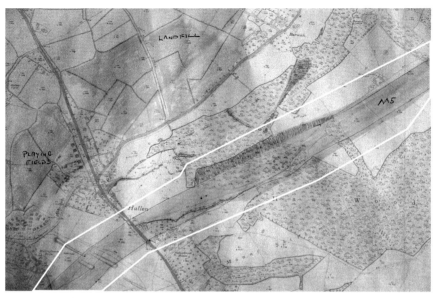

The route of the M5 showing the countryside lost beneath.

An aerial view of Berwick woods (in the foreground) showing the route
of the M5 with Spaniorum hill adjacent.

Image credit: Britain from Above 1944

Wildlife Park 1971 (Credit, Nick and Dee)

Golden eagle.

Fuzz the fox.

Sannox the red stag.

Sear the kestrel I trained.

Wildlife Park 1971 (Credit, Nick and Dee)

An eagle owl.

Dick, one of the Common seals.

Sika stag in velvet.

red kite.

Cross country course building

PR building a fence.

PR busy at work.

A new bank fence under construction.

The same bank being jumped.

A finished combination fence in Lancashire.

Another combination fence being jumped at a horse trials in Oxfordshire.

Stewarding at Gatcombe horse trials. Jane and friend Madeleine enjoying the day.

Woburn Park

Mr. Talbot, centre, on one of his regular trips caring for the herds. With him are his assistants, Mr Paul Rutter, left, and Mr. Ian Brennan.

From left PR, Ian, Dennis.

One of the Elephants with keeper Carol

Herd of red stags.

A fine red stag at feed.

Herd of Pe're David's deer
(stag centre in velvet).

The kale cut daily for the
morning feed.

Pe're David's deer at feed in their valley in the park.

An abandoned Chinese water deer fawn that I hand reared.

Berkeley Park

The park overlooking the River Severn.

Parkwall cottage.

The red deer herd 1975.

The Comeley part of the park in 1975 showing one of the
conifer plantation blocks.

Leather Craft

Some of the leather items I have made for friends.

A carved leather panel inspired by my time at Berkeley.

Exmoor 1975

The Troy Lorry in which William took the horses on holiday.

Out on a ride and looking over the dry landscape from the Punchbowl.

Exmoor BBQ evenings.

Views over Cloutsham Ball.

Badgers at Woodchester

The unfinished mansion in the valley.

A tagged and tattooed badger to be fitted with radio collar before being released.

Chris with a sedated badger.

2 cubs ear tagged and ready for release when they wake up.

Ampney Park

Jason the dog helping out feeding the deer in the deer park. A young oak sapling behind me was planted in 1982.

Jason with his friend the Manchurian sika calf.

The same tree in 2018 that I planted in 1982.

The Ha Ha being constructed.

The lakeside view of the ornamental trees and shrubs 6 years after being planted.

Yateley Country Park. 1989

Country park sign.

Heath restoration work.

Old oaks around the heath.

Volunteers helping clear scrub.

Some of the rubbish that was regularly dumped on the common.

Electro fishing the carp pond to check their condition and numbers.

Morden and NT 1992-95

Photo shoot of the haycart with Renco the stallion up front.

Some fascinated children dipping for water life in the river Wandle.

The stables and coach house with the restored clock, the building
is now used as a cafe.

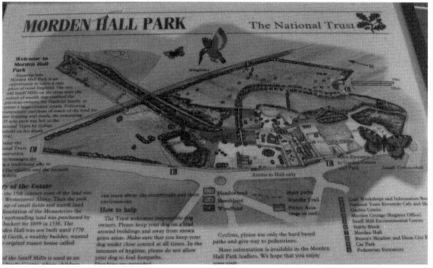

Plan of the park.

A compilation of activities in the park

All the fun at the countryside fayre.   The ornamental bridge over the moat.

Hay making in the meadows.

London Wildlife Trust volunteers hedge laying in the park.

Cheshire Countryside 1995-2002

Styal village just a mile from the new runway.

The woodland edge and fields above the Styal estate before
the runway was built.

The earth removal during construction.

The similar view after completion.

A composite of tree cutting and soil excavation

This collection of pictures shows the extensive loss of large trees and soil
required for the runway construction.

NT newsletter front page

Credit National Trust

Reports of the runaway impact and work being done by the
Cheshire countryside team.

Gloucestershire Countryside. 2002-2011

Ebworth farmhouse our home for 8 years.

The adjacent old apple orchard.

A view across beech woods
above Sheepscombe.

A Belted Galloway, one of the
conservation herd, with her calf.

Rodborough Common view from
Selesly Common.

Newark park, a view over the valley towards Hawkesbury Upton.

Woodchester Park

A photo looking west up the valley.

A view looking east down the valley before conifer removal.

Felling along the middle part of the valley.

Woodchester park, the grazed meadows looking east along the valley.

The boathouse and surrounding lake and view revealed after thinning of trees.

Conifer extraction in progress.

The Cheshire countryside team 2001.

The late David Morris.

Julian Prideaux centre with the late John Workman centre right at Johns party.

The late David Jenkins helping us out at
the country fayre.

My wife Jane.

Michael Claydon with
the restored weather
vane at Newark Park.

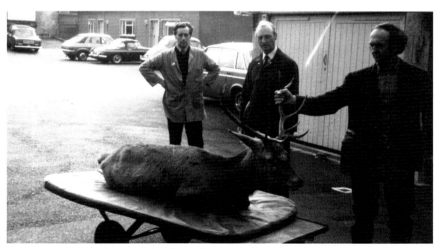

Mike Hill with a stag (under sedation) at Langford veterinary hospital.

France

The house and courtyard.

River Gartempe.

Typical Landscape of the Limousin region France.

A Pearl bordered
fritillary butterfly
on wild flowers.

Bee beetle.

Longhorn beetle.

Modern farming environmental impact

The frequent run off from fields under intensive farming.

The impact on the landscape from modern farming practice producing
food for the supermarkets.

The march of the poly tunnels across our countryside slowly being covered in plastic.

A yellow and degraded landscape.

Example of a connected landscape.

Examples of trees that have the architecture/form and space to grow to full maturity and beyond

Dawn.

Spreading beech winter.

Beech in summer.

An ancient oak forest as nature designs it.

A recruit ancient tree of the future.

Deadwood component is just as important as the living trees.

Various publicity and interpretation literature produced for some of the countryside sites that I have managed

CHAPTER 11

LAND ROVERS AND EXMOOR DAYS

I have used Land Rovers for my daily work for many years and have always enjoyed driving them. In fact, I became such a fan of Land Rovers that I decided to buy one of my own and in 1976 found a blue Series 2 registered 500 CHP, it was sitting forgotten and very unloved in an orchard in Hillsley, Gloucestershire.

The next few years saw me plunge far too much money into restoring this vehicle including: replacing new back and side-chassis members, a rejuvenated engine, gearbox, shock absorbers, new brakes, doors etc., etc., etc. Looking back now I feel it was still worth it. I had great fun driving around the lanes and using it to build more cross country courses in my spare time.

Chip as it became known served me well and found itself

in places including, Gatcombe Park, Woodchester Park and on trips up to Badminton the Cotswolds and as far as Exmoor until reluctantly I sold it to a friend. I think it is still going strong today.

Exmoor days

Back to 1975 and speaking of Land Rovers, while I was still working in the Thornbury area I became involved again with the local horse riding fraternity. It was at this time that my local riding club organised a riding holiday to Exmoor.

This sounded like a good idea, my interest and limited knowledge of the moor was thought to be useful so I joined the team of 12 riders including my mother who took their horses. I went to see the deer and my enthusiasm for off-roading!

William the neighbouring farmer of the riding school I mentioned earlier, was a larger than life character who loved fast cars, boats, HGV lorries, Jeeps and Land Rovers. I got to know him when visiting his farm as part of the badger work.

Being a big-hearted and charming character William offered to transport all the horses from north Bristol down to Exmoor in his newly acquired MAN diesel lorry. It was double unit horse box with shining varnished wooden coachwork with an attached trailer. It had capacity to accommodate 11 horses in comfort. This massive vehicle looked big enough on the motorway, so imagine the challenge of manoeuvring it through the narrow lanes around Exmoor.

It certainly startled a few caravaners along the way but everyone arrived safely and we looked forward to having a great time exploring the moor during the hot summer of 1975.

On our arrival that first evening we put up our tents and settled the horses into their temporary stables. Everyone was tired but I threw out an offer to take anyone interested to the woods the next morning at around 5 a.m. to see deer! This suggestion was met by groans of derision however I was nevertheless joined by a few bleary eyed campers next morning intent on seeing some deer, for which their early morning start was rewarded.

Each morning that week we were greeted by a pink light colouring the patchwork of rolling fields with silver strands of mist, draping the oak woodland in the valleys below. The deer would be found against the earth banks surrounding the fields, grazing on the wet grass while soaking up the early warm sunshine. I made sure the breeze was blowing in our direction so we could make our approach quietly and watch the animals from just 75 metres away, giving my friends a close a encounter with Britain's largest wild mammal that they had never seen before.

Later that morning on hearing about our enjoyable experience I was to take almost all the other campers to see deer during that week and to see Exmoor at its best in the early misty summer mornings.

During the day the riders would go off trekking while William and a few others who came without horses would go off-roading, finding hidden tracks to explore and disappear down into the deep wooded combes, crossing rivers and doing things that today, we think of as very non PC, because since that time so many people have also taken up a similar pastime but sadly many have been irresponsible and caused a lot of damage in the process.

In 1976 following the success of the previous year, another riding holiday was arranged, this time staying in the grounds of a mutual friend of William's who he had known when he lived on Exmoor some years before.

1976 was another even hotter summer than 1975 with beautiful long sunny days followed by deep red sunsets colouring the wooded valleys below purple moorland. We explored more isolated places in the Land Rovers, spending the warm evenings sitting around barbeques recalling our adventures that day.

It was during this holiday that William introduced me to Jane, my wife to be, although I did not know it at the time!

Jane was the PA and general factotum for the owner of the house in whose grounds we were staying.

We first met in the large kitchen. William had just introduced me to the owner and his family that morning and we were sitting around the large kitchen table drinking coffee when Jane entered with cucumber rings covering her eyes! She was suffering from over-indulgence the previous evening. Despite feeling rather fragile we hit it off immediately. We spent a memorable night later that week in the local inn the Royal Oak which would be shut to non-locals after 11:00 pm; no one could leave or enter and the party would continue early into the following morning. Reluctantly at the end of the holiday due to her personal circumstances at the time Jane and I had to say goodbye and I returned to Bristol.

I have an enduring love of Exmoor after being introduced to it when taken on a caravan holiday to Porlock Weir at about eight years old. This wild landscape on the edge of the Bristol Channel, with some remaining heather clad upland moorland, deep valleys or combes and fast running rivers, the steep slopes are clothed with ancient gnarled oak woodlands. The mystical light is unique here and is a place to still see a timeless landscape shaped largely by man, Exmoor ponies and the deer.

My two favourite areas of the moor are Horner woods looking over Webbers Post and opposite Cloutsham Ball, out to the English Channel, and, further south, the Barle valley. These are magical places to spend time and to watch the wild red deer in an almost primeval landscape.

Deer hunting was once part of day to day life on the moor and the debate over the wisdom of banning hunting is still ongoing. We often stayed with friends at Cloutsham Farm, which was once a hunting lodge for the Holnicote estate. I remember seeing the stag hounds running across the hill chasing after deer. I was never sure if the most suitable candidate animal was hunted when compared to my experience at Woburn because I think the larger heads were favoured by the hunt, rather than the weaker animals. It is something I shall never really know now.

Before the ban however I tried to learn more, I went out one early morning with the Harbourer; I read a book about the harbourer once so was really interested to meet one. His job is to find the best animal to hunt on the day. It is reckoned to be a job needing a 40 year apprenticeship. After a short time stalking across some moorland to find deer we soon found some, and were looking at animals which, compared to animals we would have culled in a deer park, did not seem ideal for hunting. However I was sure after all his years as Harbourer he knew what he was looking for. Over the years the deer I saw on the moor were mostly in good condition and had well-formed antlers, so it seemed to provide good results.

I know from my own experience that if wild deer are too numerous and allowed to dwell in places for prolonged periods, they will cause severe damage to trees, crops and undergrowth. So the hunt served a valuable service in keeping the deer on the move and well scattered across the moor. This was in sharp contrast to deer protection groups who had sanctuaries on the moor, which alarmingly became areas where I understand disease was rife, and overgrazing caused serious intestinal worm problems.

A few months later back in Gloucestershire, I spent some time in the autumn with William at his cider farm making what else but cider. We went around nearby orchards collecting up all the apples and using original and very old pressing gear that was still in working order in his barn. Long canvas belts and an assortment of gear wheels criss-crossed under the low barn roof which all came to life as the grey Ferguson tractor outside was fired up and attached by yet another belt through a hole in the wall.

I will never forget the noise and smell of the old tractor

TVO exhaust, mixed together with the scent of the sweet apples. The clattering and whirring machinery slowly increased in speed and the building vibrated as it pushed the 'cheeses', all piled high on a wheeled dolly, against an enormous wooden beam. The golden liquid was squeezed out of the apple mash which poured down pipes into the barrels assembled along the barn wall. It made some pretty potent stuff after maturing for a while, so I did not try much but it was very popular with the locals.

After the holiday that year I continued to spend time travelling around the south west in my Ford Escort, including making more holiday visits to Exmoor.

The following year, in 1977, on my way to see other friends who were staying at Withypool on Exmoor, I called into the place we stayed on holiday to see if Jane was around and still working there. It was haymaking time and I found her busy working in the fields helping out the tenant farmer. The chemistry between us was still there but we were still unable to get together.

Later that day I continued on my way to Withypool to meet with my old friend Diana who had a longstanding boyfriend now and was staying with Frances at her family's holiday home with its commanding views overlooking the village and the Barle Valley.

Being on my own, I rather gate-crashed this happy party of couples but was warmly welcomed by all.

I remember spending much of the time chatting with all the assembled couples and this continued late into the night when just Frances and I remained downstairs enjoying each other's company again after such a long time. I left early next morning saying goodbye to Frances through her bedroom door. It was the last time we met.

Because I loved Exmoor over the forthcoming years I was to try on a number of occasions, without success, to find work with the National Park and the National Trust. In the coming years I was to attend interviews for two jobs, head ranger and a ranger for the National Park and then again some years later with the National Trust for the property manager post at Holnicote estate. However it was not to be.

Meanwhile in Gloucestershire I continued to enjoy the research work in the Cotswolds doing bait marking operations for the next few years gathering more useful information about badger ecology.

After another three years with MAFF the six-monthly renewable contract finally came to an end. I moved on from doing the badger work and began seeking a new adventure.

CHAPTER 12

A TWIST OF FATE

Out of work again and at a loose end – then quite by chance, having returned early from a trip into Bristol, the phone rang to hear my farming friend William's voice. He invited me to meet him in a pub where he had some mystery guests that he wanted me to meet. On my arrival at the White Hart pub in Littleton on Severn I was very surprised to meet Jane from Exmoor who I had not seen for three years. She and a girlfriend Trish were staying with William doing some interior decoration for him at the farm.

Jane's circumstances had now changed, she had left her partner, a farmer on Exmoor and had moved to Cullompton, she and Trish were decorating houses.

The attraction between us had not diminished and we got to know each other again but even better this time! More good news, I learnt that she was a trained cordon bleu cook so my earlier introduction to good food would hopefully continue. She was still living in Devon with friends Carolyn and Tony who later welcomed me into the family home on my regular trips down to Devon to see her and enjoy her company and her good food.

Living at home again, I was unsure of my next move but as fate always has a way of doing so, it took an unexpected turn. The scientist I worked with at Woodchester on badgers, had set up a new piece of research work and invited me along to discuss it.

With my thorough knowledge of the work site and of the local badger population, I was subsequently employed to track each night a few special individual badgers fitted with radio collars around the research area using the radio telemetry and night vision equipment.

One memorable evening stands out when I was watching these badgers. I was out on a very dark night with no moonlight, wearing layers of warm clothing and armed with all my gear, which included a heavy pair of night sight binoculars, a radio receiver a box the size of a small biscuit tin and an radio aerial with four antennae. I also had a flask of hot drink and used a shooting stick to sit on.

I had walked along the top of the valley in a cultivated field above the woods and found a spot to sit and watch one of the radio marked badgers we called Glenn, he was foraging nearby. As I sat there in the darkness looking through the night sights I had a strange sinking sensation and felt as if I was descending downwards. I tried to stand but realised my legs were stretched out in front of me and I was in fact sitting flat on the ground with the shooting stick embedded feet deep beneath me. Such was the weight of all the gear that I had to carry around and walk through the undergrowth in darkness, without making any sound in the pursuit of the badgers.

Around this time Jane had moved from Devon and up to Gloucestershire to the small village of Colne St Aldwyn where she had previously worked for a short time after leaving the big house on Exmoor.

During the week and because much of my work was done at night I was living in a small caravan that I had purchased a few years earlier. It was a useful base for me to work from, situated at the top of the park, overlooking the valley and the rather spooky looking derelict mansion below. The park was about 20 miles away from Colne so when I wasn't working I would commute across to spend time with Jane and get to know the locals.

One evening I decided it was time to introduce Jane to the badgers in the valley, so before dusk on one very cold November night I took her to the Beech Tree sett where there was an observation platform built up a large beech tree. I gave her firm instructions not to make a sound and stay very still.

Despite living on Exmoor, Jane was not known at the time for having a rustic side, she did not even have proper walking boots in her a shoe collection, so venturing down into a steep woodland at dusk was a somewhat challenging moment for her. We climbed onto the platform and we sat quietly for some time as the light diminished from the valley while keeping our eyes firmly fixed on the numerous entrance holes below us of the enormous badger sett. We soon saw some nocturnal activity and watched a very lame and possibly three-legged fox wander across the field next to the wood. Then a tawny owl began screeching in a tree very nearby. Slowly a crisp bright moon rose over the valley rim, illuminating the mysterious and rather forbidding outline of the gothic mansion in the valley below us. In the moonlight we could now see a little more clearly the entrance holes of the sett, where I was hoping to impress Jane and show her a glimpse of the black and white striped head of a badger. After a couple of hours of waiting in the darkness and having not seen or heard anything I reluctantly decided to return back to the caravan for a hot drink.

I slowly began to descend down the ladder back to ground level when Jane told me that she could not move. She had become so cold that she had frozen to the spot! Eventually after vigorous rubbing of legs and arms she was able to return to terra firma and we marched briskly up the track to gain some temperature in her stiff body. She had passed the initiation test but unfortunately not seen a badger!

This is an all too common story of badger watching but I hoped it had not given Jane any second thoughts about me, having experienced a rather eccentric way of spending a *romantic* evening together.

Then winter arrived and in 1982 it was a very bad one indeed. I woke up early in the caravan to find deep lying snow over three feet deep outside the door.

It was obvious that work had to stop until the blizzard

subsided and the snow thawed. I decided to get to Colne somehow? The village had a very popular pub called the New Inn, and was the centre of all social activities where we spent many enjoyable evenings and Sunday lunch times, so a it had to be the best place to be in a blizzard. All roads were blocked with snow but I decided to make my way to Colne, over 20 miles away!

Optimistically, I struggled through a freezing gale up the hill to where my car was parked but Plan A quickly failed as I could not find my car; it was buried deep in the snow!

Plan B – I returned to the caravan in relative shelter of the valley and decided to drive my Land Rover into the valley and find a sheltered route along the valley to join a road and then drive onto Colne. Annoyingly, I very successfully buried the Land Rover only 300 yards down the track entering the valley!

Returning again to the caravan I embarked on plan C. I clad myself in layers of warm clothing including a lime green balaclava and walked through the raging blizzard to Kingscote, the nearby village about four miles away. After a couple of hours I reached the Hunters Hall Inn and where a friend Reg lived in the house next door. I was able to ring Jane from there. Although the roads were almost completely blocked with snow and deep drifts, Michael a good friend living near Cirencester, agreed to attempt to collect me in his Range Rover and I was successfully rescued and decanted to the New Inn in Colne having first stopped off in Cirencester to collect supplies for the village. The scene in the middle of the town was surreal, the cars were all gone and replaced with horses tied up to some trees while their owners, who had come from somewhere out of town were also stocking up with supplies.

I remember on reaching Colne all the occupants of the pub coming out onto the snow-covered road to cheer as we came down the hill. We were the last vehicle into the village for the next two weeks!

The pub was a friendly buzzing place in the heart of the village with a diverse clientele ranging from locals, millionaires, authors, entrepreneurs and pilots, farm contractors and frequent holidaymakers enjoying a weekend out of London in the Cotswolds.

Mark was the landlord, he amongst many others became great friends and often visited little Japonica cottage where Jane was now living while the owner Noel a pilot friend worked away in Switzerland. Japonica became the focus for many memorable social Sunday lunches with often up to 18 people enjoying great food, local ale and not so fine boxes of cheap wine!

One memorable lunch, we had a suckling pig cooked in the oven at the pub because it was too big to fit into our Aga and we transported it up the hill to the cottage in the back of a model A Ford! It had to be one of the best meals ever.

Time at Woodchester went quite fast, spending many nights following radio collared badgers around the woodland and fields and soon enough the two year contract with the research section of MAFF came to an end, so I was unemployed yet again and began to enjoy a brief life of leisure in the Cotswolds while looking for a new challenge.

Having some time available again and known by the local horse fraternity, I was approached to build another cross country course near Malmesbury and was also asked to be the chief fence steward at the new Gatcombe horse trials, so I enjoyed some great horse trials and social gatherings in the grounds of some beautiful estates.

Back in Colne, Jane and I continued to meet more locals and establish a diverse and very special circle of friends. Derek was an RAF pilot, Rupert was an ex-agriculture-college student and drove tractors, Jonathan was another new friend and he was an antique dealer who had recently moved down from Cheshire and one evening in the New Inn he introduced me to his father Tim.

Tim had just purchased a large house with grounds near Cirencester. A little later and after a long chat about my experiences in conservation and with animals as well as my love of the countryside, he asked if I would be interested in working for him and running his newly acquired small estate.

I had not seen the place but it sounded a very worthwhile project as the business plan for the property was to become an event venue and centre for nature conservation.

I visited the park to look around and thought it had great potential to become a perfect place for all his and perhaps some of my ideas, so I accepted the offer to restore and manage the park grounds.

The house was to be completely refurbished so no one lived there for the first three years apart from the builders from Cheshire who camped in the kitchen.

During the first few years I got on with a lot of the hard landscaping and reshaping of the park which had become neglected including thinning old conifers, re landscaping the parkland and lakeside with trees and shrubs, felling and planting more trees.

I have visited the park recently to see many of the trees thriving some reaching a height of over 30 feet.

Tim regularly visited from Cheshire but left me to get on and implement my plans so this was a rare opportunity to put some of my ideas into action, designing a landscape and looking after a historic park and garden. It gave me a secure job while also learning about plants, trees and a lot more.

While at Ampney Park Tim, who was a generous man, offered Jane and me a dog. Jane's black labrador, Charlie, had recently died and Tim's family had bred some more Labrador puppies born at Tim's home in Alderley Edge. The parent dogs were both chocolate and the current local fashion then was to own chocolate labs which meant the right colour pups would be a lucrative market. However all the puppies turned out black or yellow so were unable to find good homes in a fashionable area, so one of the black pups was given to us and he enjoyed a great life as my right-hand dog. We called him Jason.

On moving in to the park we inherited a flock of Jacobs sheep at Ampney. Sheep are renowned for wanting to die from birth so I had to constantly attend to various ailments. They were hard work and had to be shorn by hand. I thought they just did not look right in the small paddocks so I suggested to Tim that we open up the area to become one large space and introduce some deer. It had once been a much larger deer park and remnants of the original park boundary wall could still be seen.

Re-establishing a deer park

Establishing a smaller deer park involved removing yards of old post and rail paddock fencing, then erecting 6'6" high-tensile perimeter fence, much of which would be hidden in new tree planting. This task involved a lot of hand digging into the solid stony soil for the straining posts and then excavating a ha ha in front of the house to give uninterrupted views. The deer that I thought would suit the parkland location would be Manchurian Sika from Asia, they look impressive and were straight forward to manage.

I managed a herd of these deer while at Woburn, so I knew their characteristics and temperament. We visited a collection of these deer in Sussex and were able to purchase four animals, one stag and three hinds, from the owner. When the deer were settled in a month later, I introduced Jason the dog, bucket in mouth, to the deer and he would join me to feed them each morning, all got on very well together. A year later Jason struck an interesting friendship with a calf that he grew up with – it was hand reared after its mother had abandoned it. Both of them would run circles around each other in play. (It is of course not recommended for wild deer to have dogs running around them and they should always be kept under close control in the presence of deer and other livestock.)

This was however a very good introduction for the young dog to get used to seeing deer for when in future we would venture down to Exmoor.

A year or so after starting at the park Jane and I decided to find a house to rent together so we left Colne and moved a few miles away into a farmhouse outside a village called Southrop. It was an old, very pretty, but very draughty house and full of flies.

One memorable day the following summer I very clumsily cut my arm badly after pushing it through the window of my little caravan, while pushing it out of the way to let a farmers' tractor pass in a narrow lane. This meant a few weeks in hospital and I received many stitches this time; silly me!!

Fortunately my arm was very well stitched back together and I was able to continue using all the usual tools of my trade including the chain saw.

Another year later as we both felt pretty secure in our jobs and we both loved living in this area, we decided to get onto the property market. Ideally a small cottage with a nice view of open countryside would have suited us well but as the prices were so high we bought a new modern house well described as a "box" on the edge of Cirencester.

Although I had always resisted the idea of being married or having children it came as a great surprise when I suggested to Jane that we should get married. After the initial shock she thought it was a great idea and said yes.

Our wedding ceremony was a very quiet event in Cirencester, witnessed only by our dear old friend William and his wife Sarah. We wanted a quiet affair without contentious guest lists or following any of the usual protocols. It was however followed by a trip to Exmoor which was a weekend with glorious frosty mornings and blue sunny skies. We were spoilt by William who booked us into a luxurious hotel for a night, before celebrating our marriage with a group of somewhat surprised friends who we had invited down to join us in a rented cottage but knew nothing of our wedding. They certainly did not expect to be celebrating our honeymoon with us!

Over the following five years I made good progress restoring the park and I achieved a lot, establishing a wood pasture, planting a shelter belt of trees and restoring wetland, landscaping the lakeside with trees and shrubs, maintaining the formal gardens.

I was helped by Elaine who taught me a lot about plants and young Simon, a keen angler just out of school and determined to start a career in the open air despite poor guidance received from his school.

A range of birds of prey arrived together with two young falconers who Tim employed to pursue his interest of breeding endangered species to replenish wild populations and to also fly birds for the public at the park.

Unfortunately after six years all the exciting plans for the park came to an abrupt halt with the untimely death of my boss Tim. Although very wealthy he did not seem a happy content man and died one evening at the park, very sad.

Following Tim's sudden death I needed to think what I could do next to keep paying the mortgage. Fortunately on learning that I was looking for work, I was asked by a fencing contractor I knew to build him cross country courses for his clients so the following months I travelled around the country building jumps for events and for private individuals. It was hard work but it kept me very fit and was a lot of fun, but it was not a long term career move.

At the same time I was told that there was the possibility of a warden job arising at Sherborne Park, north of Cirencester with the National Trust. However, fate was to intervene and due to a new Regional Director coming on the scene the position sadly never materialised, although I got as far as being interviewed and looking at the lodge that was to be the accommodation for the job.

I attended numerous interviews around the country over the next few months. I have lost count of just how many I attended. All this upheaval and uncertainty, quite apart from the stress, must have had an effect on my confidence, although I was not aware of it at the time but being rejected time and again is not good for anyone.

CHAPTER 13

YATELEY AND OTHER COUNTRYSIDE

Finally a job at Yateley Common came my way after yet another interview, and by June 1988 I was working as a Head Ranger for Hampshire County Council Countryside department. Yateley is in the far north east of Hampshire, squeezed between main roads, an adjacent runway and housing. We moved to the Ranger's house which sounds impressive but this was a mid-eighties brick house sitting below a busy main road on the edge of the common. John my boss was based at a distant office so he gave me a pretty free rein to manage the country park, a lowland heath SSSI with lots of challenges.

I settled into this role very easily and felt it was the type of job that I had been seeking for many years.

Soon after I started I was approached by a journalist for

the *Times* newspaper who had heard of my recent arrival and background and thought it would be worth interviewing me to learn how I had so far pursued my career in the countryside. It was to be an article for the education supplement and I explained to the reporter how important I thought it was to obtain practical experience rather than rely on academic qualifications for this type of work.

I had two full time staff initially at Yateley, who were both very set in their ways but welcomed me and showed me the ins and outs of the place and it soon became clear that the common was a hotbed of problems from illegal motor biking, fly tipping, boundary disputes, and heath fires in summer. Although a designated an SSSI (Site of Special Scientific Interest) there was even a large metal recycling yard in the middle of the common, and we had regular visits by travellers occupying the area in their caravans, always leaving a lot of rubbish behind them. Although it was a valuable and protected open space many people saw the common as a waste ground which could be abused and desecrated.

With the impending retirement of one of the rangers I was soon able to employ a new young enthusiastic chap called Paul, and he made a big difference in the work we could embark on including getting the local community involved in caring for the common. Few local people seemed to appreciate that it was an important countryside site needing sensitive management, in what was a busy, developed part of North Hampshire and was one of the few remaining rare lowland heathland sites in Europe where special plants and insects clung on to survival. This was also habitat for rare silver studded blue butterfly.

The common was persistently abused pretty well every day and night.

The first job to do each morning would be to collect the rubbish left around the site. Almost every day we filled a transit van full of rubbish. Tyres, fridges and building materials were constantly being dumped. The council also spent many thousands of pounds cleaning up after travellers who despite being evicted at great expense returned again and again!

It was a challenging job but worth doing and was an opportunity to restore the heather by removing birch and pine trees and scraping off the grass and humus. This would encourage the heather seed to regenerate which preferred poor mineral soil and plenty of light.

Many local people enjoyed visiting the common in the evenings and at weekends. It was their green lung on the edge of the concrete urban fringe. Schools would visit to learn about the habitats and our conservation work.

The endless daily routine of clearing up other people's rubbish, removing stolen cars and continually repairing the damage done by vandals showed me the contempt that many humans treat our green spaces.

Fly tipping has become epidemic proportions across the country today indicating that this significant problem is still very out of control.

Working for the water company

After a couple of years having acquired more good experience at Yateley and the opportunity to study part time for a Certificate in Management Studies, Jane and I were both thinking of our next move. We were missing real countryside and we yearned to move to somewhere like Devon. I also thought that by staying in one place could limit my career prospects and I was still young so I was seduced by an advert for a Recreation Controller with a newly privatised water company.

This was during the Thatcher government years when private enterprise was king and the public utilities became private companies with shareholders. This particular water company had acquired a contentious reputation caused by the pollution around the coast and a major incident at Wadebridge. The company was under great pressure to reform, to make money and to fully embrace privatisation.

The job as Recreation Controller was intended to give the company a greener image regarding the environment and to develop its skills in recreation and countryside management.

The area I covered would include the whole of the south west peninsula stretching across Devon, Cornwall and some of Somerset, Exmoor and Dartmoor national parks, Bodmin moor and surrounding areas. Part of the new job was to help change the status of reservoirs as they became water parks for wildlife and be used more for recreation as well, so my job was to retrain the existing bailiff staff and to be more like countryside rangers. What was not good to like?

The reservoirs were tucked away in valleys across rolling landscapes; places like Siblyback, Colliford in Cornwall, Wimbleball on Exmoor and Fernworthy on Dartmoor. The mighty Roadford Lake had also just been completed after building a dam across the River Wolf which, during the construction revealed some ancient secrets including an old water mill when archaeologists explored the place before the water inundated the valley.

The next year however was unfortunately to become my "anus horribilis".

My boss was a feisty, hockey player and liked to be in full control all the time. I had to share the same office so I was often interrupted in mid-telephone conversation to be informed what I should say! My correspondence was also checked.

My duties were wide ranging and became an ever growing list including:

- To produce detailed conservation management plans for all the surrounding land, around 9 reservoirs, now renamed water parks.

- Attend meetings, day and evening, across the three counties, including various fishing federations.

- Produce interpretation material and respond to press and public enquiries.

- Oversee fish stocking, and visitor health and safety.

- Manage staff and produce a handbook for the new Ranger team.

- Implement a training programme for the Rangers.

- Maintain good relations with all colleagues and adjacent landowners.

■ Plus many other duties as new recreational activities were being introduced.

Pretty soon after starting the job I was being pushed to the limit and was finding it increasingly difficult to split my time between the office and visits to the sites, which I thought I needed to get to know and survey properly.

I was eventually instructed to spend less time out on site! My agreement with the lease hire car company had a condition to drive 12,000 business miles a year which became increasingly unrealistic so I could not see this situation working out too well.

I soon began hearing comments from other staff and how few people could work with the new practices and processes being introduced by the company and by certain individuals. Some disenchanted staff began leaving the company as they reached desperation point with their jobs. I challenged my boss on a number of issues but was fruitless as I apparently had no right to suggest ideas on different ways of doing things.

I was getting a feeling that my conservation background was being used to give a positive, green image to the company and that environmental best practices was being promoted while wider development ideas by the company were being explored at some prime locations around the south west.

After eight months doing the job I was also becoming increasingly concerned about getting a bad reputation and losing my integrity and my sanity. It had become very clear by now that this was not the job for me so I began looking for work elsewhere and was invited along to an interview for the Head Ranger post at Exmoor National park.

It raised my hopes to be asked to attend an interview. All the candidates had to do some psychometric tests and we all received quite a grilling, only to be informed in the end that although I had performed well, I had not been successful and the job was given to one of the existing ranger staff.

I was thinking that it would be such a shame to leave glorious Devon but it was looking increasingly as if that would have to happen. Then my hopes were raised once again when, quite surprisingly, I was invited to attend another interview for another ranger job on Exmoor. This one would be replacing the now newly promoted ranger from the earlier interview. However I was informed again that I was not successful this time either.

This job went to a seasonal ranger who had worked there for just three months. I really don't think they should have invited me back. Although this was an odd episode I think a senior member of the park staff was hoping to introduce new blood to the long established team.

After more months of persevering at the water company trying to maintain my sanity, working all hours of the day and night, trying to achieve unrealistic targets and driving to meetings around the south west peninsula in a little Peugeot 208, I eventually reluctantly decided that enough was enough and I resigned.

So it was goodbye to that sorry episode, I understand things have changed significantly in the way the company manages the water parks since my departure.

I had now come to accept that fate was not on my side for me to remain in Devon or to work on Exmoor, so the hunt continued for another job elsewhere.

Over the previous months I had applied for other jobs outside of the area and I attended interviews at Epping Forest, the Peak district the Mendips and two jobs in West Sussex and in Surrey with the National Trust.

Meanwhile we continued living in our little village in our cottage that we had renovated into to a cosy home in mid-Devon enjoying the friendship and support of the locals.

Jane was working in the nearby Technical College so I had some time to think what to do next.

While working for the water company, Jason the dog had not been at all happy, having to stay at home all day, rather than accompany me to work. It was sad to watch him slump with a groan into his bed as I left him to go to work each morning. Now at least without a job we were both able to enjoy the area more together and spend my free time enjoying the glorious Devon landscape, walking across Exmoor, spending time with our friendly neighbours, farming friends and spend time watching deer, badgers and the bird life in the wooded valley below the village.

One evening we were walking around a field in the valley near the village, I was looking over one of the Devon banks with a hedge on top when I spotted some red deer on the other side of the bank. I bent down and began stalking them to get a closer view. Jane stayed behind but as I stopped a little further on to look over the bank. Jason was following behind me and copying me by stooping as he walked and crouching down as he followed me. A prime example of a dog and his master working together in harmony. A very special moment. Jane was in hysterics watching this strange spectacle.

CHAPTER 14

NATIONAL TRUST DAYS

After the less than enjoyable experience with the water company I wanted to return to a more practical outdoor job again.

I had well proven practical experience and broad knowledge about land management and ecology acquired over some years now, together with a determination to conserve our countryside.

I had also got to know quite a lot of National Trust properties around the country and I still thought they were the type of organisation that I had been hoping to work for one day.

As I mentioned earlier, some years previously I had been seriously considered for a job with the National Trust at Sherborne Park in Gloucestershire.

A few weeks before leaving the water company, one of the many jobs I had applied for was in Surrey as a Head Warden with the National Trust. I had not heard anything from them so assumed I was not a contender.

I felt at the time by joining a well-respected conservation organisation would be the right career move, so I was very glad to receive a letter from the National Trust inviting me to attend an interview for the job in Surrey

This was great news but the date of the interview was for that very same day at 11:00 a.m. and would be held in London. It was 9.00 a.m. now and I was still in Devon! After a quick phone call the interview was rescheduled, thank goodness. Was fate on my side again at last?

Jane had said any job would be fine anywhere **except** London, so it was a little deflating for her to read the small print about the job and to find it was in Surrey at a place called Morden Hall Park in South London!!

On the day of the interview Jane and I drove up the A30 in the October sunshine through increasing amounts of heavy traffic, in contrast to the quiet lanes of Devon, then onto the M3, under the M25 and into the suburbs of Kingston, Raynes Park, to Merton. The noise of modern life assaulted our ears, steel, glass and concrete immersed us, the mayhem of a fast moving world all around left me wondering if this was such a good idea.

On our arrival at the park we entered a very contrasting environment. Set behind a high red brick wall an idyllic lost landscape appeared, sitting on both sides of the slow running River Wandle with its network of serene backwaters. Along the drive the half clapper-boarded miller's cottage came into sight, this went with the job and would be our new home. It was just feet away from an old water-powered snuff mill, this had provided the original source of the wealth that created the park.

On our arrival we met David Jenkins, he was a little younger than me, he was the land agent who would be conducting the interview. David had a big job, he was responsible for this property as well as a number of other estates across southern England that he managed for the National Trust. We seemed to be kindred spirits and immediately got on well. I also met the two rather mature resident wardens, they were both quiet stern looking gentlemen, and had been maintaining the place for some time. It has to be said they were a strange couple and they would prove to be a challenge to manage.

When we returned to Devon we noticed how quiet it was. That evening David rang and offered me the job which I accepted, although Jane was not too impressed.

Sadly, David died quite suddenly in 2016, it was great shock. We had been great friends as well as colleagues. I am very grateful to him and he is greatly missed.

Peter, a friend from Devon, helped me to move up to Morden later in October 1991 by. This would be a time to get to know the place before the outgoing Head Warden had left. I stayed temporarily in a house built in the perimeter wall on the edge of the park. The walls were wafer thin and the busses on the main road stopped outside very frequently rattling the floors and windows as they arrived and left. The air stank of fumes, police sirens whistled passed at high speed almost every half an hour. This was civilisation?

The next few weeks I gradually got to know the people in the Trust and explored all corners of the park, a mixture of hay meadows, mature trees, a wilderness area on an island and formal grounds including a rose garden. A large garden centre and a new National Trust café had just been built within the walls of the old kitchen garden. The River Wandle that ran through the park was once the only trout river running north from the North Downs but it was now an outfall for a large sewerage plant. It had a rank smell about it and most unpleasant things were often seen floating past. The park grounds were adjacent to a high-rise council estate often used by *The Bill* police television drama for location work.

The park may have been an idyll but it was surrounded by a pretty ugly and forbidding piece of suburbia. Some of the locals I have to say were not your average National Trust supporters, looking rather surly and menacing, covered with tattoos, always walking at a purposeful pace with head down. Some were accompanied by a bull terrier type dog breathing heavily and straining on a metal lead, with heavily studded collar and harness. Some of these animals, I later learnt were trained to hang off low branches of trees in the park to strengthen their jaws! Someone said it was for dog fighting.

I later came across frayed lower branches of trees all around the park and I thought what a way to treat a tree.

Before I arrived in 1991 the park had previously been a mothballed site and pretty well shut down with a liberal use of barbed wire and high locked gates in an attempt to restrict public access to some parts of the park. The National Trusts focus in those days was much more on the country estates in the shires and not on the inner city properties.

After a few weeks Jane joined me and we moved into Mill Cottage where my predecessor had lived before moving on to Box Hill. Mill Cottage was within the park grounds and much further away from the main road. From here you could not hear the noise outside the park which was muffled by trees and the sound of the rushing river water cascading over an adjacent weir.

Although it sounds a perfect location it did mean that by living on site I would be responding to all manner of incidents day and night, although no overtime was paid.

We regularly saw people clambering over fences and the high entrance gates to take a short cut, or sometimes to steal something. I had to get streetwise pretty quickly and adapt to a very different situation now many miles from the quiet rusticity of Devon.

Yateley and its problems were looking strangely familiar again! As I have already said, one learns from practical experience and my time at Morden was to be an experience.

This was a place where late at night we would regularly hear a helicopter hovering low overhead, the house vibrating while its spotlight was directed into the grounds in search of a suspect on the run from a crime that had occurred nearby. The local rogues often used the seclusion of the park as a sanctuary in which to hide.

Police were regular visitors and often called in for a cup of tea while telling me about the exploits of some of the nocturnal locals. On one occasion very late into the night we were woken by a commotion outside the cottage and looked out of the window to see a police officer pushing a squeaky wheel barrow with a flat tyre, very odd we thought. Odder still was that it had a dead coniferous tree sitting in it! The policeman saw us peering around the curtains and asked if I could look after the wheelbarrow and put it somewhere safe, just so it didn't get stolen again, he laughed! It had been stolen from the adjacent garden centre together with various other items and found abandoned.

Despite such incidents, there were a lot of good and very positive things happening as well at the park, it was becoming more welcoming and popular to visitors. It slowly became a jewel for the local urban dwellers who were able to enjoy the river running through the hay meadows and walk under fine old trees.

This was in complete contrast to the noisy surroundings outside the wall and it was not uncommon to hear woodpeckers, see herons and even the occasional kingfisher darting along the water courses. We even had stag beetles living in the ancient trees in the meadows.

The old snuff mill building had a classroom upstairs and was used as an environmental study centre for visiting school where Mark the teacher introduced and captivated urban school children with a hidden natural world; this was a rare opportunity for them to explore a piece of countryside that they had never seen or experienced before.

We promoted the following mantra to all the children who visited:

When in the countryside take nothing but time and leave only footprints.

Later I used this perfect venue to run an evening class on nature conservation for the University of the Third Age.

I soon realised that the two wardens had their own very rigid routines that could not be changed easily in what they did and how they did it. Due to the park being mothballed for years, they had enjoyed their own freedom to do much as they pleased and had, up to now, enjoyed a very low profile in the Trust.

The park was developing fast, so old traditional ways of working had to change. The new garden centre, tea room and craft units had just been completed and opened to the public. It took some time, but change happened. I think that I gradually convinced them that I had some good ideas so, as I got them involved they became more enthusiastic and a little more supportive.

A gentleman called Gilliat Hatfield was the original owner of the Morden Hall estate, which was once much larger landholding. He once owned many more acres beyond the park boundary wall and was a wealthy and successful businessman, making his fortune from the snuff milling industry.

Although he doggedly resisted many threats to his land, much of it was eventually lost through compulsory purchase for housing development. However, he prevented the core part of his estate being built over by giving it to the National Trust in the 1930s, together with a large endowment.

During his life Mr Hatfield resisted new agricultural techniques including the use of chemical herbicides. His far-sighted environmental concerns conserved the plant rich meadows in the old deer park. He also used horse drawn vehicles up until the 1930s to transport him into London to meetings.

We have lost 90% of our hay meadows around the country today, so their conservation has become vital to maintain biodiversity and to help lock up carbon. As I got to know the park better I decided to terminate the fortnightly grass mowing and let the grass grow. Soon after I found an incredible mix of traditional grasses and herbs growing in these meadows. Ox eye daisy, birds foot trefoil, goat beard, sorrel and many more plants also appeared and flowered. Butterflies and bees flittered across the warm grassland in summer.

I purchased second-hand hay making machinery and began restoring the hay meadows. This meant cutting the grass in late July after the flowers had set seed, baling it up and getting it quickly removed before some of the locals could throw the bales into the river or burn it! The insects living in the grass were still able to hide in long grass left uncut around the margins of the meadows that I called sanctuary strips.

To publicise the change of meadow management we were successful in having and an article published in the *Guardian* about the restoration of these all too rare hay meadows. We needed to get the story to stand out and be different so we borrowed a black Friesian horse called Renco and put him between the shafts of an old cart that we had in the stables. The photographer from the *Guardian* came out and was able to take pictures of this very rural scene in south

London. It made a good article for the paper and it gave some great positive publicity for the park and the Trust.

The NT also decided to publish an article about my work at Morden for their magazine. Some weeks later I received a postcard from the editor; by coincidence the postcard had a photograph of someone who I was to meet and work with some years later.

A country fayre called "Countryside Comes to Town" was our main event each year at Morden, it was jointly organised with an events company. This was a lot of hard work but great fun when everyone got dressed up in period costumes. It was held over the Spring Bank holiday and attracted up to 30,000 people. We were able to set up a much larger National Trust exhibit which promoted countryside and rural skills. At that time the Trust had its own team of tree surgeons working in the region so we were able to include one of the warden's real passions, trees and tree surgery. Over the years the team had accumulated a chamber of horrors of bits of wood showing bad practices done to trees. Brian, one of our wardens, was one of the team and loved explaining all this to the visitors. Sadly, the tree team was later disbanded.

This event really put Morden on the London map and many people living in the city got to know more about National Trust by visiting the show.

Other responsibilities I had at the park included conserving and enhancing the historical landscape and buildings in the park, managing the visitors, tenants and overseeing the security of the 57 roomed Morden Hall that had become vacant shortly after I arrived.

I became the caretaker of this building for two years while it sat empty, responding to numerous false fire and burglar alarms, usually at night, until finally it was taken on by Whitbread pub chain. They extensively renovated the building and opened it as a pub and Beefeater restaurant.

Jason the dog was the world's biggest coward (he took a torch in his mouth when we let him out for a pee at night on Exmoor) but he was my essential company for me when checking the building, giving me a feeling of false security.

Despite his timidity he settled in well to his new life at Morden, escorting me each day while I carried out my duties. He also became a useful ambassador often helping to break the ice with locals and visitors, some of whom preferred to say hello to him rather than to a strange human being.

Another project I embarked on at Morden was desilting of the moat around the main house. To do this we imported huge dredger that pumped the silt into pre-dug lagoons in the northern end of the park and left it to dry before being buried.

The northern part of the park was devoid of trees because part of it had once been used as a landfill site, of all things. The built up ground was made up of ash, poor and compacted soil, a newly planted shelterbelt of young trees did not grow well to begin with so to remedy this I thought I would try a company that had special equipment to aerate the soil by injecting compressed air and dried seaweed around the tree. It had miraculous results and the trees have grown well since this was done.

Watermeads was another NT property I managed, just a mile up river, and as the name implies, was originally a water meadow. Helped by the Wildlife Trust volunteers we restored the network of water rills around the site and fitted a new sluice gate to control water levels, paid for by the National River Authority, to establish a new wetland.

It is now used as an example of best practice in wetland restoration and is one of the first sites to be restored along the River Wandle for water vole reintroduction. It is a haven for birds and acts as valuable stepping stone for wildlife along the valley.

A new City Farm was also built on Trust land to the north of Morden Hall and was opened by HRH Prince Charles. Morden Hall Park has become an acclaimed location for nature and for people as a wilderness site within a cityscape. It is a piece of remaining rare countryside in greater London just a few miles from Wimbledon. The River Wandle has continued to be cleaned up after some serious pollution events and has plenty of fish in it again. The local community love the place. Gilliat Hatfield should be proud of his generosity and foresight.

I hear there are plans to designate London as a *National Park City* with all its green spaces, of which Morden Hall Park is a prime example of how important such places are for people and nature within a city.

Alarmingly crime and violence was always present at Morden and Jane and I both had a few nasty experiences when people became threatening, and on one occasion a young man even came into the house when Jane was there alone. As

I mentioned earlier our dog was not a good guard dog.

On another occasion early one evening we happened to glance out of the window when the park was closed, and we saw two individuals carrying some familiar looking cane back chairs past the house which we suspected had been taken from the craft workshops. We rang the police thinking they could intercept these lads but we were told that they were far too busy dealing with a stabbing to attend. Very frustrating. It turned out the chairs had been stolen from one of our craft workshops.

Although I tried to stay positive and with this and many other incidents including losing Jason to cancer after five years at Morden I had reached burn out stage, so I began looking for another position in the Trust.

While living in London it had presented me with a perfect opportunity to fill in some gaps about the theory of countryside management which had at last now been recognised as proper vocation and profession. So supported by the Trust I signed on to a Diploma course in Countryside Management at Birkbeck College near Russel Square.

Returning to academia and doing assignments, meeting like-minded people, having discussions and debates was an interesting experience. I thought some of the lecturers had pretty strange perceptions about our countryside though. I did get good marks for my assignments and after a delay finding a tutor to complete the course I finally received my certificate confirming my achievement, by which time I had moved on from Morden northwards to another National Trust job up to Cheshire.

Escaping the city to Cheshire countryside

After leaving Morden Hall Park ideally I would have liked to have stayed in the south of the country and been able to use my experience in one of the many jobs I applied for there, but was not offered any of them.

After yet more interviews the next job I was offered was a Countryside Manager position. This job was managing all the open space properties across the county of Cheshire and included a whole village and ancient buildings. Despite my good track record and clear commitment to the organisation, I still had to go through formal interviews which were very demanding but I was able to convince the senior management that I had the necessary skills, commitment, knowledge and knowhow and that I was fit for the job. Even after being offered the job, I still had to meet the Regional Director for his final approval!

This job was much bigger and even more challenging than my previous one in many different ways.

The warden (Ranger) team I would be working with in Cheshire were a larger team of nine people, plus an office assistant. There was also a hard-working team of people on a job creation scheme. They were all keen to work outdoors and learn about nature conservation. They were another mixed bag of characters but all had a real passion to look after the countryside.

The Trust had some fine dedicated staff however they had been very closely regimented by my predecessor so it took a while to give them the confidence to make decisions of their own and to even voice an opinion.

The job was based in Styal village at the estate office. The property is probably better known for the Quarry Bank Mill below Styal village set in the Bollin valley, it was then owned but was not managed by NT.

As well as the mill the original village and the Styal estate had over 30 houses with private tenants, a dairy farm, a small church, a chapel and a village school.

The other properties I was responsible for included some spectacular countryside, Alderley Edge, a sandstone ridge with its extensive copper mines adjacent to Hare Hill park and garden. At Nether Alderley a unique sixteenth-century corn mill built within the dam that impounded water to power tandem water wheels. A millstone grit outcrop called the Cloud above Congleton gave commanding views. Further afield was Helsby Hill and Mow Cop Folly (a weird place). On the west side of the county it included Bickerton Hill and later the adjacent Bulkeley Hill on the beautiful Peckforten Hills was added after we were able to make a strong case for the NT to buy it in 1998. Altogether I think we had the best viewpoints in the county.

Initially, much of my time was taken up managing the Styal village and estate but gradually other NT administration staff became more involved allowing me more time to concentrate on the other open spaces.

Meanwhile the traditions continued within the village. Each month some of the village tenants filed into the office to hand over their rent and have a chat, or moan about their house or their landlords, just as they had done for many years before.

A year into my job I had a new challenge to deal with. This was the £175 million new second runway development at Manchester airport. It was right on our doorstep and its construction was finally approved after a planning enquiry at which the NT objected. The NT had been the only objectors at the public enquiry, very concerned at the devastating effect this construction would inevitably have on the river valley, woodland and adjacent landscape. Few other local people seemed to appreciate or even care about the impact that it would have on the area.

As the local property manager, I became the main representative for the NT to try to make sense of what was a "design and build" scheme and liaise with the airport staff and their contractors. Being so close to the Trust property, a condition of the runway planning permission was to give the NT some influence in trying to minimise the impact as far as was possible, on the trees that would be within just a few feet of the new runway perimeter. There was a surprising absence of regional and head office staff at this crucial time, when I would have thought their involvement was pretty important.

Tree protestors, including the infamous Swampy, were, we were told, already in the adjacent trees and had dug tunnels where some remained right up to the time when the actual work started. Some moved on to Trust woodland a week before work actually began on the trees affected by the runway. It was intriguing how the protestors were always very well informed about the airports plans.

I had some interesting discussions at first with the protestors who invited me to join them in the trees, although it was tempting to support them it was not how the NT did things!

Later some more hardline protesters arrived and these needed to be treated very carefully.

To construct this brand new runway over mile long was to be a design and build project but I am not sure this was fully appreciated during the planning process. The result was that drawings and calculations had to be redrawn after the public enquiry. This all resulted in the runway eventually being constructed 15 metres lower than the existing ground level. The depth at which it was to be built depended on the engineers calculation of the amount of soil needed to fill in the adjacent Bollin Valley that was to also have a tunnel built over it.

This project involved huge amounts of soil being excavated across an enormous area. They even tried to relocate and conserve some ancient woodland at great cost. It did not work.

Such extensive ground work, combined with very heavy rain over the following three year period, put the whole valley and our woodland under great threat. Even a road between Styal and Wilmslow had to be closed and then removed. This was a loss that did surprise and upset the locals.

Although some trees on NT land would not be felled, many would have to be reduced in height but this depended on where the trees actually were under a zone called Obstacle Limitation Surface (OLS). With changes being made to the levels almost every other week, I spent many hours with engineers, ecologists and contractors on site and in the project managers offices, to discuss and agree the best solution that would minimise the damage to the woodland and how best to manage any bad press that both organisations would be receiving if things were not done as was originally agreed.

The country's press and TV eyes were on us.

At the start, we were given assurances that each tree would be treated individually and would be coppiced or pollarded as the NT requested, depending on their species and location under the OLS. We stipulated that no vehicles would be allowed within the woodland and large sections of tree would be retained in situ as decaying timber.

Although a lot of good quality timber had still to be removed the NT saw little financial return because much of it would disappear in the early mornings by unscrupulous timber merchants.

We lost fine, mature beech and ancient oaks, stately ash and yew trees in this operation. All were irreplaceable yet with our endless thirst for flying to distant sunny beaches the general public seem happy to see this destruction happen.

As the NT were to acquire the land on the perimeter adjacent to our woodland, we saved the airport money by redesigning the bridleway to replace the lost road, we proposed a more natural and safe alternative to the steep gradients and tight angular bends originally drawn up the for planning permission. Without my intervention this would have been constructed. It appeared that the engineers found it difficult to design features that would suit horses, cyclists as well as walkers and that would blend well into the landscape.

The construction of Runway 2 at Manchester illustrates the continuing unsustainable threat to our landscape created by such large developments. HS2 is now looming and is yet another major threat to our remaining green and pleasant landscape.

Runway 2 has changed a rural part of Cheshire out of all recognition forever by removing every natural feature from what was once a rolling green landscape. Despite all the claims that it was needed, there is still a question over this. The original runway infrequently seemed to be really busy before Runway 2 was built. Planes were not being stacked and now Heathrow says it also needs yet another runway.

If we forget what has been lost to build the runway this destruction will only continue in the name of progress and growth. We all need to remember this loss and consider if we can just sit back and watch it continue.

Despite clear and irrefutable evidence of global warming, the negative impact of burning oil, atmospheric enrichment and affect from cloud dimming, we continue to demand to fly all over the globe.

Witnessing the destruction at Manchester I have chosen not to fly. If I can manage without using planes, then I am sure plenty of other people could at least reduce their need to fly. If we all readjust our life priorities and lower expectations by living with a lighter touch on the planet, we may perhaps see it survive and we and future generations can all enjoy a better quality of life.

We once adopted something called the Precautionary Principle but it is seldom mentioned or used these days. We really do need our politicians and planners to adopt this approach and to think longer term!

I think education and the media has a vital role to play here, to be less focussed on narrow curricula subjects and targets. Instead it should inform and broaden our understanding about the environment giving everyone, young and old, an opportunity to learn about nature and the impact we are having on our environment. We need to promote a culture that is better connected to our surroundings and work together for the best long term interest for all of us. We must consider future generations more and their quality of life.

One positive that did come from this depressing runway saga at Styal was the acquisition of Northcliffe farm and fields adjacent to Styal Country Park. The airport gave this farmland to the NT as recognition of the irreparable damage done elsewhere on the estate. Here we were able to restore the hedge margins and ponds before the farm tenant took on the tenancy, so we have made sure there was room for wildlife. The regional NT newsletter reported this and other work that we were doing around the county.

While in Cheshire one of the wardens I worked with needs special mention here. David Morris was someone I developed a great respect for and have great memories of working with him at the Bickerton Hill where he was the warden. David very sadly died in 2014. He was dedicated, spirited and very capable warden (now called ranger) for Bickerton Hill, Bulkeley and Helsby Hills on the west side of the county. He spent most of his time there on ambitious projects to restore Bickerton Hill back to lowland heath and enhance the biodiversity of adjacent woodland.

With support from Darren, an apprentice ranger, David also recruited many volunteers and inspired them to transform Bickerton Hill from being an overgrown birch and pine woodland, once used as a firing range, to become a rare piece of lowland heath in west Cheshire with far reaching views across to Wales.

Welsh Black Cattle and later Exmoor ponies were introduced to maintain the rich habitat that he worked so tirelessly to restore.

We became great friends as well as colleagues and between us we convinced the NT to acquire Bulkeley Hill just up the road from Bickerton. We should remember David and thank him for all the work he did to restore Bickerton and Bulkeley including gathering tons of sandstone from nearby fields to rebuild steps, paths and the perimeter sandstone wall.

Other successes I oversaw while in Cheshire included; stabilising the eroding escarpment at Alderly Edge, using a horse to thin Scots pine from lowland heath at the Cloud near Congleton, building a topograph at the summit and restoring one of the waterwheels at the old mill.

Because of yet more internal NT restructuring I was relocated from the office in Styal into a Portakabin at Alderley Edge. This was quite a change to my surroundings of Styal village estate office and my next challenge was to build a new office building and replacement workshop which I helped design with an architect. It was a disruptive time for the staff but we got there in the end. I think the building not only looked good but also functioned well, set under the trees at Alderley Edge.

The move from Styal required Jane and I to leave the NT accommodation in the village, which was just half a mile from the new runway and we were able to purchase a house near Macclesfield and a few miles from the new office. We were very glad that we were able to afford it and move just before the new runway was about to open.

After moving to Blackberry Cottage we decided it was time to have another four-legged friend having not had the company of a dog since Jason died in London six years earlier.

We found a black Labrador retriever in of all places Gloucestershire, he was born down the road from Ampney Park where I used to work many years ago.

On our first introduction to the dog owner we had to answer some rigorous questions that she asked all her prospective puppy owners, which was a good thing. Having passed the selection process to have the puppy she soon pleaded with us to collect him to give his mum some peace! A week later we collected our nine-week old pup, drove him up to Cheshire and decided to call him Bracken.

Bracken was a bit of a thug when young but he soon became my right hand dog, coming to work with me and finding a quiet place under the office desk, waiting patiently until his next walk around Alderley Edge, or a visit to Bickerton Hill to see his new great friend David.

I continued managing the Cheshire properties for a few more years but always kept one eye open for other work opportunities in the south as we were both missing seeing the rich flowers in the meadows and the golden sunlight across the hills of the south west. It also seemed to rain an awful lot in Cheshire!

To make our intended move simpler we sold Blackberry Cottage and rented what we thought was a delightful converted smithy near Henbury Hall. It actually turned out to be the coldest house we have ever lived in, that winter Jane used to cook supper wearing fingerless mittens, a woolly hat and boots because the north wind came up through the floor and howled under the kitchen door. One weekend a friend stayed and he slept in a sleeping bag on a camp bed in front of the fire in the sitting room. In the morning when we went in with his cup of tea, he was blue with cold —we thought he had died of hypothermia in the night. Fortunately it was just a year later that we were on the move again.

CHAPTER 15

TO GLOUCESTERSHIRE AT LAST

I anticipated being in Cheshire for around five years before moving on. However, after applying for some other interesting management jobs, it was eight years before I was able to move on to another worthwhile job with the National Trust. I had applied earlier for a countryside manager post for Dorset but was pipped at the post by Helen, another countryside manager. In the end it worked out well as Helen was given the job, so she moved from her existing one in Gloucestershire and moved down to Dorset. I then applied again for the now-vacant post in Gloucestershire, which I had been interviewed for a few years earlier. This time I was offered the job as Countryside manager to look after all the open spaces owned by the NT around beautiful Gloucestershire. HOORAY!

This was a great job and we could now move back to what I call real countryside. It meant living in a Trust house again and was one of the real benefits as I saw it of working with the N.T in those days. This time it was an isolated old farmhouse high above Sheepscombe village and located at the end of a mile long farm drive.

The estate where I was based included the countryside offices for Gloucestershire. They were above the old stables and workshops for the nine-strong ranger team in the surrounding old stone barns. John Workman was the original owner of the estate and he had an office there having generously gifted most of Ebworth to the NT and he continued to influence the affairs of the estate. By strange coincidence John was the person featured on the postcard that I received from Sarah Jane the NT magazine editor while in Morden over ten years ago.

John lived in a cottage in the valley below and we met regularly so we got to know each other well and spent time talking about the estate and its history, about trees and the National Trust. John was closely connected with the Trust for over 60 years during which time he was a forestry and nature conservation adviser. He was very generous to the people he knew and as a local donor my job was to keep him informed about estate matters.

John was a highly respected, forthright gentleman with strong opinions but despite his sometimes controversial views and his high expectations for the estate, he was a fount of knowledge on innovative forestry. He died some years later but I am very glad I knew him.

I also had a wide range of other challenges that the job presented. This included managing two large commons both with grazier and advisory committees, producing a conservation plan to restore the lost formal landscape of Woodchester Park, the same park where, by coincidence I worked on badger research many years ago.

The badger research at Woodchester had continued but following its acquisition by the NT the Wooodchester Park landscape had changed since I worked there in the 1970s. It had begun with the removal of many conifers at the western end of the park and to restore meadows in the bottom of the valley. Installation of dam spillways on the five artificial lakes was under way to comply with reservoir regulations.

We produced a landscape conservation plan for the park which included opening up views and restoring more meadows and create wood pastures along the bottom of the valley.

Just down the road near Wotton-under-Edge I also managed Newark Park, another property with its stunning views towards Hawkesbury Upton and 600 acres of valley woodland and sheep pasture. Michael was the custodian of the house. He was a delightful charming and charismatic man who, when his partner was alive, together they restored the interior of the house. Michael later took on the role of custodian to manage and entertain visitors to the house. My job as well as supporting Michael was to manage the surrounding landscape with the ranger team. In February, I remember spending many hours in the cold directing visitor's vehicles to a field we used as a car park, they had all come to look at the impressive snowdrop display.

Such was the setting of the unchanged farm buildings at Newark that a film company used it as a location to film *Tess of d'Urbervilles*. This posed an interesting dilemma over the safe use of candles in the tithe barn. Since losing buildings to fires the Trust policy was not to allow any naked flames although eventually it was possible to get special permission to allow candles to be used.

On the west side of Gloucestershire is Westbury Court garden the unique Dutch water garden and Ashleworth tithe barn is further north on the banks of the Severn. Both were included in my portfolio of properties. I also looked after the imposing May Hill which dominates the landscape for miles around on this side of Gloucestershire with magnificent views over nine counties, just a few miles from my home near Ross-on-Wye. I often visit it today.

Sherborne Park near Northleach was one of three properties that were later added to the list of open spaces I was to help manage as part of an evolving countryside manager role in Gloucestershire.

Sherborne was the estate where I almost got a job as warden many years ago when the NT were planning to appoint a warden but things changed following a review by a new regional director. It's a funny old world.

Nearly 20 years since leaving the county I was now leading a team helping to manage 8000 acres of National Trust owned open space land and properties across Gloucestershire, much of it a protected landscape within the Cotswolds AONB.

It was very satisfying for me to be able to manage what were already familiar places to me having grown up in the area and I soon introduced Bracken to them who always looked forward to his trips out with me when I made my property visits.

Similar to my work in Cheshire, I needed to work with wide section of the community including landowners and house holders, graziers and commoners, farm tenants, schools, councillors and other organizations including councils, planning departments, the Environment Agency, Natural England and many contractors.

Living in Laurie Lee's landscape

The Gloucestershire farmhouse we lived in was a delight. It was an old stone building situated high up on the Cotswold escarpment not far from the Slad valley, the home of the late author Laurie Lee, author of *Cider with Rosie*.

At 950 feet above sea level we experienced our own weather system at Ebworth. There was an average of a one degree difference by ascending just 200 feet more above the nearby village which meant we had snow while others below us had rain, so we were often snowed in. Most winters the snow would blow across the long entrance drive making drifts feet deep, cutting us off for a few days until Martin, our friendly tenant farmer and neighbour, was able to dig us out. We had some very cold but pretty winters in 2008 and 2009.

We loved the solitude away from people and roads, and it was the perfect place for the dog. We also enjoyed many supper parties and barbeques in summer with friends while looking across to the apple orchard where the Belted Galloway cattle had their calves and where the occasional roe deer grazed peacefully on the sweet grass.

Laurie Lee would recognise this place today and the wildflowers that still grow there.

The farmhouse itself was basic and idiosyncratic, wrapped around the original stables and coach house of what was part of the original hunting lodge of Ebworth house, that had fallen down. The farmhouse was once lived in by Dennis the original farm manager for John in the 1950s and who still lived on the estate. He was now a beekeeper making honey from numerous hives scattered around the surrounding farms.

Despite the isolation and cold winters, it was great fun to live at Ebworth and my previous life of living in Park Wall cottage many years before proved very useful. My wife Jane also felt at home having lived up on Exmoor for a number of years.

The NT owned a herd of Belted Galloway cattle for grazing and browsing the scrub on steep slopes around the Cotswold escarpment and keeping the SSSI's in favourable condition. The fields around the estate were farmed organically by Martin the tenant farmer. He was a jovial character and regardless of the weather always had a cheery smile and a chuckle despite the challenges of farming on this high and exposed ground.

Being so isolated the water supply was tapped from a spring in the woods in the valley below and pumped up to a reservoir above the original house using a water pump called a RAM. This is an ingenious invention that does not need any power source, although on our arrival to the house the RAM had been replaced with an electric pump and bizarrely reliant on a diesel generator, so I thought it made sense to resurrect the RAM and decommission the smelly diesel/electric pump.

With a little effort and modest expense we got the RAM going again. It uses its own water pressure from a spring to pump water long distances. These ingenious pumps are still widespread and used across the country. You can still get spare parts from the original makers by using the unique serial number that each pump is given.

The RAM did require regular checking and the sand and UV filters were also regularly replaced but the system was reliable all the time we were there. We did of course have to be wary during drought periods.

Sadly, just before I left, the RAM was again decommissioned, which in my opinion was for no good reason, and was replaced by a mains water supply, paid for at great expense by the NT. The new supply was brought across farmland from a mile away, and was apparently to satisfy a health and safety concern that from our experience of enjoying fresh and unadulterated water was not justified. There were originally three RAMs in the valley which had supplied water to all of the estate over previous generations.

As the weather became cooler we soon found that the farmhouse had a defective oil fuelled "wood" burning type stove that one night we were unable to turn off and an even older coal-fired Rayburn that only worked when the wind was in the right direction! The oil stove was removed and later the Rayburn replaced with a central heating boiler. A new proper wood burning stove was installed and we used home grown trees from the woodland below.

A few years later the extensive resource of local wood was put to even more good use when we installed a new heating system to heat all the buildings on a district network, heated by a state of the art 75kw wood boiler. It heated the offices and workshop complex. It was also backed up by solar panels for heating water in the summer. This project was made possible through a heating grant and went towards the NT target of 20% overall reduction of its carbon emissions.

Below the house on the steep valley sides grew over 300 acres of mixed woodland including many fine beech trees planted by the donor's father and later by John himself, who was renowned for his permanent cover forestry technique. Permanent forestry meant trees are removed one by one, retaining surrounding canopy of trees but allowing enough room for new recruit trees to grow tall and slender up to the light, often reaching 30 feet tall before the first branch. Premium timber was produced for the furniture trade this way. As fashions changed less beech has been in demand so today many of these trees will be felled for other uses including wood fuel.

Before the Trust took over, John's loyal forester Dave did all the tree thinning, by measuring the girth of each tree first and always ensuring that another tree nearby would be able to replace the one he felled. Dave was one of the last remaining true woodsmen I knew who understood the trees, the woodland and the wildlife that lived there.

Underneath the beech trees there some special plants still grow that he and John cosseted and are protected there today.

We often walked through a landscape of grazed commons, small farms with dry stonewalled boundaries and thorn hedges. The mellow stone cottages with small windows and steep rooflines gave the place its unique character. Colourful meadows and commons still remain here rich in wild flowers, butterflies and insects conserved by the sensitive grazing. Now confined to just a small parts of our countryside and surrounded by large arable fields and dense blocks of under managed woodland.

CHAPTER 16

THE FRENCH CONNECTION

Living in the farmhouse at Ebworth enabled me to carry out my daily duties more effectively. It meant I could walk just a few yards to the office, keep a check on the estate at all times and ensure the security of the buildings. Having sold our house in Cheshire it seemed pointless for us to just own a property that we did not actually need. We also had a bad experience of letting a house previously, so we took a chance and acquired a farmhouse in the Limousin region of France. It included land, some woodland and a river frontage, something not possible to have ever considered owning in England with our limited budget.

This all came about in 2002 just before leaving Cheshire when we went off on a three-week camping trip to mid-France. This was a place we had never been before and we came across a glorious old farmstead for sale in the Limousin forest area. It was big leap of faith but we thought we would regret not taking this opportunity of owning such a lovely property. Having made an initial visit early in the holiday we returned three weeks later on our way back to England and while sitting under an old pollard lime tree in the sun baked courtyard, we decided it was by far the best property out of all the others that we had looked at across the region, so we put in an offer and it was accepted.

The farmhouse was owned at the time by a tall Frenchman who had lovingly renovated it with new roof, floors, windows, tiling and all the services had been updated, although the plumbing was very French!

The house was set on a south facing hillside with views across an endless forest of sweet chestnut trees and oak, interspersed with small fields and the land farmed as it would have been in the 1950s in England. The place was vibrant with birdsong of golden orioles, nightingales, redstarts and many insects including stag beetles hovering precariously over us in the warm evenings. There were also chafer beetles, grasshoppers, lizards, butterflies and much larger wildlife all thriving in the grounds that surrounded a range of old barns and small outbuildings. We had numerous bats in the barns, salamanders were found under stones, red squirrels were in the trees and so much more. It was true countryside and one that we have largely lost back in England.

The River Gartempe ran along the edge of one of our woods; it was part of a specially designated Natura 2000 site.

Kingfishers, heron, wagtails and deer were all seen regularly.

Bracken spent as much time as he could swimming in the water and always remembered his way through the woods down to the river, even after some months since we had last visited.

The warm summer evening air was filled with the sounds of cicadas and bullfrogs. We saw so many insects including a praying mantis that was perched one day on the back door. Purple emperor butterflies were on the gravel in the courtyard and we listened to nightingales in surrounding scrub. As darkness fell, we could see the glow worms signalling beneath the bushes emitting their green light.

During the summer months the front of the car was often smothered with insect corpses that collided into the radiator grill as you drove along the lanes. This was something you once saw in Britain as well. Their absence is an ominous sign.

The woodlands we owned were in four separate blocks of mixed oak, hazel and sweet chestnut. In the garden was a walnut tree producing delicious nuts most years. I used the chestnut for cleft fencing, for structures around the garden and to keep our enormous wood burner (the most inefficient one I have ever known) burning on the colder nights.

Looking at how the landscape in this part of France has evolved could provide some clues as to why in the UK our countryside is so much quieter and has such poor biodiversity.

The average size of a farm in the Limousin is quite small, many farms are carved out from the large mixed forest that is still managed by the local people. The irregular shaped field margins around the woodland merge gently into a mix of rough grassland and scrub while other fields are separated by lines of trees and by un-flailed hedgerows. Few of the fields have been improved or land drained, other than having a ditch dug around the perimeter. Numerous small ponds and lakes, natural and artificial, are common and well scattered, fed by brooks and streams. Livestock are herded regularly along tracks and through woodland to adjacent fields. Something we rarely do anymore in England.

The woodlands and hedgerows of trees are managed for both timber and for firewood, producing fencing and building material used by the farmers and local builders.

The local hunt manages the larger animals including boar and deer, although the hunters reputation can by no means be described as perfect and they did tend to shoot anything that moved including humans! However, they did keep wild animal populations scattered and on the move, while reducing both numbers and the damage done to crops.

The motorways that now snake their way through the French departments have specially built green bridges over them, designed specifically for wildlife to link forests and the wider landscapes together. This allows for the free movement of wildlife.

Maybe we have some lessons to learn ?

All change at home – again!

Back in England in 2010 and due to yet another reorganisation foray by the NT, I had to reapply for my job again which, thankfully I was successful in retaining, so I was very, very surprised in 2011, without any warning, to be made redundant after working for the organisation for nearly 20 years.

During all the time of working with the NT its staff seemed to be going through constant and relentless restructuring of some form or other. It must have been very expensive to the Trust and was very unsettling for the people affected.

For reasons that are still far from clear to me, some senior and relatively recently appointed NT managers had decided that they did not see the need for a countryside manager anymore in Gloucestershire and preferred to use my salary for a business development post!

With this devastating news we thought long and hard about our next move. Should we stay in England or move permanently to France and set up a "glamping" business making a living by using and sharing our beautiful environment. We explored all the practicalities in depth but decided in the end that the bureaucracy and a poor enterprise culture as well as our isolated location could not support the business model, although the local Marie supported our idea. Also in our part of France most local amenities and even tourist attractions were pretty well closed for eight months of the year! Our potential clients would have found it difficult to find places to visit.

We had owned the house in France for nine years, it was an experience not to have been missed, but with the loss of my job we decided that we had to sell it and say goodbye to France.

By now I had accepted that it was time for a change and I said farewell to a splendid team of people who I had enjoyed working with. I was saddened that the National Trust had changed so radically over the past few years. I enjoyed the opportunity of working for the Trust that I had devoted twenty years of my life caring for and managing special places for the organisation and for its visitors.

It was also a privilege to live in the Cotswolds and to have had some influence in the management and conservation of such rare and iconic places, I really hope it stays that way.

Although change can be good, to discard so many passionate and dedicated staff with experience and knowledge seems a very short sighted policy which I am sure the NT will eventually come to regret.

It is hardly a surprise therefore that at the 2016 AGM some Trust members raised concerns over the distinct lack of communication and countryside skills on its properties. The Trust now has had to rely on external advice and use volunteers. The question is: Who mentors, trains the new staff and volunteers now?

Reflections on 20 years with the NT

The National Trust was born in the mid-1800s out of similar concerns that we still have today about our environment, seeing the impact of development, agricultural and industrial pollution and loss of open spaces affecting everyone's quality of life.

The Trust began by acquiring just four acres of land in

North Wales as it felt land ownership was the only way it could protect it. In 1907 it was able to have the National Trust Act passed that meant it had its land protected for ever for the nation.

This was long sighted and visionary at the time and the NT has grown into being an enormous organisation for environmental and cultural good protecting thousands of acres of open countryside.

I am proud and privileged to have worked for such an organisation and to have learnt so much from the people I worked with.

Sadly, many of those people are no longer there. Some were made redundant like me, others left demoralised replaced by less experienced staff who were focussed more on implementing trendy short-term popular ideas and policies; this view is echoed by fellow colleagues.

I fear such changes has done the NT reputation no good and has only weakened its once highly respected image as a nature conservation organisation in particular.

The presentation of its properties have become far less bespoke and instead cheaply popularised with numerous, brightly coloured signs giving often patronising information.

I learnt a lot from my colleagues in the Trust including the importance of knowing, understanding and respecting the history of each property before making any changes and of listening to the wisdom of local people and their fore fathers. Many good things have been done by previous generations before us and we should learn from them and from their mistakes as well as their successes and not try to reinvent ideas that are doomed to fail.

Despite it all, I think the NT is still a fine organisation with many people still there who are trying hard to do the right thing.

I am sure the NT will survive but it would be wise to change the way it engages with both its tenants and its visitors as well as with its own staff and to consider better ways to use its unique resources more wisely.

I hope the NT reprioritises its agenda and gets back to managing our landscape and threatened environment rather than seeking short term policies to compete with other enterprises who are better placed to offer packaged Disney type fun activities.

CHAPTER 17

TREES IN MY LIFE

Rather than moving from Ebworth straight away because of my redundancy, I was able to stay by agreement with the NT who allowed us to rent the house. It was a relief that we were not losing our home as well as my job.

I decided to chill, reflect for a while and to not jump into the first job that came along. To think what next and what direction I really wanted to take.

When I left the NT I was told by friends that I was not looking too good! My health had suffered probably by the top-heavy management causing me stress and reducing my ability to use my judgement and discretion. I realised that I no longer loved the job any more, sitting in front of a computer, filling in forms and seemingly getting nowhere.

Now I had the time available I busied myself getting in touch with old friends and acquaintances, reconnecting with the big wide world and throwing off my institutionalised NT mind set. I visited places that I had not had the time to visit before.

I then came across information about a woodland gathering meeting being organised by the Forestry Commission the following October and I decided to attend.

The venue was in a delightful location on the Blackdown Hills in Somerset and the whole event was beautifully crafted and organised by Gavin Saunders, we would be camping in the woodland over three days. I even met some ex-NT colleagues there.

It was the final event of a lottery bid project with the objective of re-establishing links to our woodland culture and reintroducing grazing to some of the recently cleared conifer forest. A project intended to reconnect people to their landscape.

Although we were camping, very good facilities were laid on, providing a canteen, showers and loos and we sat around camp fires surrounded by ancient trees discussing conservation, nature and people. There was wide agreement by everyone that the landscape was important to all of us and it had to be managed holistically and on a much larger scale. If we and our environment had any hope of surviving it was thought very important that everybody needed to be able to have a connection with their natural world.

This experience helped me to decide what I wanted to do next and it took me back to trees and reminded me how they have influenced my interests and career over so many years.

Returning to Gloucestershire revitalised, I became

interested in the canal restoration of the Stroud canal. I volunteered some of my time to do a survey of the trees along the route. Many trees along the canal had been neglected and were in poor condition and needed a management plan. Fortunately, a specialist team of volunteer tree surgeons were available to help me and were brought in to carry out work that would have otherwise been very expensive.

I soon became very concerned about the consequent loss of biodiversity by the enthusiasm of some of the canal volunteer team to remove trees for firewood during the rebuilding of the canal, I also thought it would be such a great loss to remove both living and some dead trees unnecessarily and that it was so important for future users of the canal to enjoy a wildlife rich green corridor.

Concrete, steel and bricks were replacing what had been reclaimed by nature. This was one of the reasons that many people criticised the restoration going ahead. I could see the restoration had potential to enhance the whole of the Frome valley for people and for nature if done well but I found a distinct lack of enthusiasm to embrace this vision by the engineering element that was leading the restoration.

Reading the most recent *TROW* canal magazine it reports the revised Lottery bid does include its intention of enhancing the valley corridor as a whole for both nature and for people, which is welcome news. Prince Charles has just opened the first six miles that has been restored so I hope the next phase will include more biodiversity along the length of the canal.

While helping the canal trust I took on a role as voluntary

Biodiversity Director where I oversaw the start of rebuilding of the Weymoor Bridge foundations under which badgers were living and in the original channel of the canal. Under license from Natural England and after a careful excavation operation we retained most of the original sett and the badgers continued to live there.

While spending time around Stroud I also got to know Stratford Park, this is a delightful open space and historic park in Stroud. It has a little known arboretum, a rare thing to have in a town. I was introduced to the manager by Steve, a friend and local wildlife artist. The park is owned by the District Council and after learning about my background from Steve, I was asked to produce a plan which would inform the next five years in enhancing the biodiversity around the park and begin planning for the future to ensure the tree collection remained an important feature.

I spent some free time getting to know the park and then produced a biodiversity plan for the park. It has a fine arboretum as well as some grand ancient oaks and all needed sensitive management. This project seemed to me to be a very worthwhile way of influencing good practice in nature conservation and land management and to use my experience, much of which had sat dormant with the National Trust for far too long.

The biodiversity plan has been enthusiastically adopted with many of the recommendations being implemented.

Mike is the grounds manager of the park and is local to Stroud. He is a fine entomologist and ornithologist and committed to implementing the plan. He sends out regular newsletters explaining what he is doing and what he is seeing in the park which includes more bird species, more insects, wild plants etc. all in quite a short time. Awards have been won following this work.

As they say, it is so good when a plan works. The park is another good example of the importance and value of green space in towns and it will hopefully go from strength to strength. It is continuing to win awards and be a place for the people of Stroud to get close to nature within their own community. There is also a nature festival organised by Steve each year. Events with a nature theme are arranged around Stroud as a celebration of nature and is a showcase event which attracts many conservation groups and visitors.

I use the park and the collection of trees to give regular tree walks, taking people around the park and introducing them to biodiversity and the magical and mysterious world of trees.

Experience comes in handy again

We continued to stay at Ebworth for another three years paying a fair rent which reflected the condition and isolated location of the house. I continued to keep a watchful eye on the buildings and equipment, lock gates at night, help to keep the wood boiler lit, check on the livestock in the adjacent fields and let Martin or the rangers know if there were any livestock problems.

I was applying for jobs, however most applications went nowhere although, notably, I was invited along to initially a first and then a second interview for the post of Superintendent of Windsor Great Park for the Crown Estate.

My experience must have stood out from my CV so I felt privileged to have had the opportunity to see behind the scenes of the Great Park and to have been a contender for such a prestigious and challenging post. The job was given to an internal candidate.

By now I had a very clear aim of becoming involved in trees again and ideally the ancient ones, having seen the impressive collection growing around Windsor Great Park. I had been closely attached to trees for over 50 years, experience I thought could put to good use somehow. So in 2012 I was very excited to see a job advertised with the Plantlife charity who were looking for a new Woodland Biodiversity Adviser.

I applied for the job convinced that my experience fulfilled the criteria for the job perfectly. I was invited to an interview and was offered the job. It allowed me to work from home, which fitted into my plan well, as I was still trying to buy a house and move out of Ebworth. We wanted to stay in the Cotswold/Hereford area.

Having sold the house in France we knew eventually that we would have to move from Ebworth sooner than later so we had been looking for a house to buy in the Cotswolds. Unsurprisingly the ones that we liked were all well beyond our budget and we could not see ourselves in a terrace house on a main road in Stroud.

It was just two years after I was unceremoniously removed from the Trust that while still at Ebworth, another countryside manager was employed to do the same job that I used to do, although it was under a different job title. How odd!

He paid us a visit one evening to the farmhouse and seemed to think that he knew a lot about the estate and told me his plans. He seemed quite convinced they would have all been approved by John Workman, the now deceased donor, although he had never actually met John.

I had known John well and I believe he would have been less than impressed with the plans to offer what was described as fun activities around his woodland. In his view, the new manager thought this was how to be an exemplar in conserving the countryside.

I think he got the message that I was not impressed.

It came as no great surprise a few weeks later, that I was informed by a NT that our rent will be going up by more than 30%.

As there was no willingness to negotiate the rent I gave the NT a month notice to quit.

Luckily, and after a lot of searching we had at last found a suitable house just in time, but regrettably it was not in the Cotswolds.

Getting a small mortgage for the new house was a nightmare. It is a long story, another book probably!

We left Ebworth farmhouse in May 2014. After our furnishings had been removed, the run down condition inside became very apparent. I understand much money was spent by the NT improving the house before eventually finding a new tenant.

Plantlife 2012

I had joined Plantlife in October 2012. It is an organisation devoted to standing up for wild plants and fungi in GB and across Europe. A founder member was Professor David Bellamy, 26 years ago. Since then it has championed the importance and value of wild plants including lichen, mosses and the kingdom of fungi. Although a small charity it has had a great influence over protection of our threatened plants and wild flower meadows attracting good support from its Patron HRH Prince Charles.

Since starting with Plantlife I visited important plant areas across the Cotswolds and the adjacent counties; some included sites I managed for the NT. I have been working with some very well-informed and professional staff and I was given the freedom to develop my new role, trusted to give advice and to run projects. It has been really interesting to spend time to get to know even more about woodland plants. Sadly one in six of our woodland plants are threatened by extinction in the U.K.

My job was to encourage woodland owners to manage neglected woodlands that we have so many of across the country. Nearly 40% of private woodland are undermanaged so by offering advice to as many people as possible on managing their woodland, not just for timber production but for bio diversity as well.

Many special and rare plants are found in the Cotswolds and Wye Valley Important Plant Areas so sympathetic woodland management is crucial to maintain both common and threatened species. One plant I became closely involved with was the Spreading Bellflower *Campanula patula*. A beautiful plant with a blue flower confined mainly to the England Wales border and a few other places. It relies on traditional coppice management to flower when the light is let in onto the woodland floor. Silk Wood at Westonbirt of all places has been found to have a thriving population of this plant following the reintroduction of coppicing some of the woodland there.

I have also become more proficient in plant and lichen identification and updated myself with the policies and politics of the woodland and forestry world. This included the Panel Report on Forestry which had just been published. It was produced at the request of Caroline Spellman MP after a very negative public response to the government's plan to sell off the public forest estate. Which was not a wise decision.

I also had the use of a very well researched report produced by Plantlife called Forestry Recommissioned, it sets out the concerns about the lack of woodland management threatening many woodland plants and highlights the many issues that need to be addressed. It is well worth reading.

The job with Plantlife has been most rewarding giving me an opportunity to use 45+ years of experience in managing trees, wildlife and landscapes. I have enjoyed the opportunity to meet and advise new people and organisations including Natural England, Forestry Commission, RSPB, Wildlife Trusts and many private landowners.

I have travelled to many special places and contributed to

projects across the country and in Wales to promote rare and endangered plant management and protection. It has included interviewing landowners about environmental schemes and the quality of advice they receive on managing such places.

It was interesting to hear the almost unanimous response from landowners that they thought the agro environment schemes were having a negative impact on the landscape, on trees, lichens other plants and wildlife.

Savernake Forest adventure

A major challenge I took on for Plantlife in 2014 was to re survey 5000 ancient and veteran trees across the Savernake forest in Wiltshire over three years during spring and summer.

To have an opportunity to survey the ancient trees in such a unique place as Savernake has been very special to me. It is probably one of the largest number of ancient trees in one place in the whole of Europe. Although much smaller today the remaining forest has existed here for over 1000 years and has seen kings hunt deer under some of the ancient oak trees. Henry VIII met one of his wives Jane Seymour at Savernake – her father was then the forest steward.

Much of the forest is a designated SSSI and is another Plantlife Important Plant Area for the rare lichens that still grow on some of the ancient trees. The Forestry Commission lease the woodland so are responsible for management of the ancient trees and the rare lichens.

The tree survey would be comprehensive and include: recording a GPS reference, tagging each tree, taking a photograph of each tree, noting the tree condition and canopy size of the trees and any associated flora and fauna seen at the time. I also assessed the level of threat that each tree was exposed to by shade and other external factors.

It has given me a unique insight into ancient trees and to better understand these old characters which are becoming an increasingly rare feature in our landscape. I hope the survey helps the Forestry Commission (F.C.) to manage these trees in the long term so that the rare lichens growing on them and the insects living in these trees can survive long into the future.

Recording every ancient tree in a large, dense forest is a very challenging task, both mentally and physically. Many of the trees had become surrounded by brambles up to three metres high. In order to tag the tree it required striding into the thick undergrowth (rather like the Monty Python sketch Ministry of Funny Walks) to reach the trunk. To give me some protection I wore reinforced trousers and heavy forestry boots, so by the end of each day that usually started at 5:30 a.m. I am ready for a long soak in a hot bath and a check that I have not collected any ticks.

While walking for many miles around the forest, an area covering nearly 3000 acres, I often recall the words of my career master ringing in my ears saying "don't expect to be paid for walking around the countryside young man," 46 years later.

I have had a rare opportunity to become totally immersed

in this forest, learning its history, observing and recording the characteristics of thousands of these trees, many over 300 years old and others perhaps up to 900 years or older.

It has helped me to try to understand better the changes that have occurred over the centuries that have either protected the trees or put them at some risk. When you have a large and unique sample such as at Savernake, it becomes easier to see the features that the trees have in common and it becomes a little clearer to begin to understand what influences the way the trees grow and how they respond to changes in their environment over a long periods of time.

I noticed how some trees were growing vigorously despite much of the tree was dead or decaying. Other trees in heavy shade had died well before reaching their prime or had been blown over. Some had fallen over but were still alive and growing well. The trees that were looking most healthy and sturdy were those in full sunlight and had long low branches, some growing down to the ground.

Some trees had dead branches at the top of the canopy but the tree was still growing vigorously. Something that is overlooked is that, over time, trees very slowly change their shape as they adapt to old age. This is called retrenchment and is something we all need to appreciate more if we are to see ancient trees reach full maturity in our landscape.

A question I regularly asked myself was, although we see that ancient trees can survive extreme weather events, wars, disease and stress, why are so many of our younger trees dying today or not reaching post maturity or are likely to reach ancient status?

I think the answer is that paradoxically we have too many trees crammed into our woodlands while too few trees are in the wider countryside. Many remaining trees on farmland are also growing close together, and others are in the wrong places. Thousands have been grown artificially in plantations and have genetics that make them unlikely to survive for as long as the naturally regenerated trees can.

What I have learnt

We may see them every day and take them for granted but if we continue to neglect our trees or manage them unsympathetically the trees we have growing around us today will not be able to reach their latter stages of life or provide valuable habitat as they enter a long period of slow decline, as nature intends.

Most of these trees are light-demanding species and their growth becomes constrained by the lack of space and light so when planted close together they have to grow a long stem and narrow canopy between adjacent competing trees to gain enough light. The resulting dense canopies can be ideal conditions for fungal infections that enjoy damp humid places with poor air flow. Ash die back disease is a fungal disease that thrives in still, damp air conditions and is a good example of benefiting by this neglected environment.

The heavy shade cast by many trees growing too close together also causes stress and prevents low branches from getting adequate light so the branches die off. The flora beneath the tree including the soil becomes cold and bare but which may well have once had an abundance of woodland plants when the woodland floor was more open to sunlight and the fungi in the soil enjoyed better conditions.

Tall flimsy stems with narrow canopies with small root plates are the result of this overcrowding, resulting in trees becoming unstable and collapsing or not having the leaf mass to develop properly.

Ivy is an additional and increasing threat. Although many disagree, there is a growing body of evidence that confirms ivy will foreshorten the life of a tree as it smothers the top of the tree, the canopy. Ivy is an important constituent of our woodland and hedgerows but it does need managing. Over the last 30 years or so the atmospheric enrichment with NO2 nitrogen oxide, a form of fertiliser out of vehicle exhaust, is absorbed by ivy which increases its growth rate. Nettles and bramble are also a beneficiary of this atmospheric enrichment. I measured the length of a single ivy stem that grew up the house wall one summer. It grew 8'2" between April and October, well outgrowing any healthy tree.

Thinking ahead

Leaving ivy to grow on trees may not only threaten the tree but could also become a very costly operation for tree owners and councils to clear up failing trees along the roadsides as tree canopies become smothered, top heavy and unstable.

I see trees are already failing and falling onto the roads for this reason. This is an example of how money could be saved by planning long-term tree management and a strategy towards fewer but more stable and resilient trees along our roads and railway margins.

Many of the longest lived trees were once found in our hedgerows, on boundary banks and in open spaces. These were called compass trees because their low branches radiate outwards in all directions. These trees are well balanced with a low centre of gravity so are stable in high winds. These compass trees were the favoured form for Lord Nelson to use in his warships. It is the natural way the tree wants to grow.

Trees are easily damaged by many factors including compacted and waterlogged soil, ploughing, livestock browsing and trampling, vehicle movements and fertilisers around tree roots.

Although we know much more today about how complex trees actually are, we still need to better understand the complex chemistry influencing their growth and the symbiotic relationship they have with fungi. We need to understand more how the relationship with these fungi develop, to know what the benefits to both the tree and the fungi are and what the best conditions are for this relationship to flourish.

We also need to be sensitive to how trees want to grow, NOT how **we** want them to grow.

The shape, age and type of tree can influence what other life it can support, this is one of the foundations for biodiversity. We need to be better at understanding the right management that will enhance and promote this biodiversity. An English oak tree can support well over 300 other species alone.

Every living thing requires its own individual niche. However we are systematically removing niches year on year when we cut off branches, remove dead wood, try to control vegetation and improve the soil. Allowing space for nature to do her own thing will promote more niches and give us great benefits.

Another key requirement for trees and woodland is to have a proper management plan. This should be not for just five or ten years but for 100-150 years. The pace of change around mature trees has to be a slow one, so we need to give more time and space to our trees and to allow slow natural regeneration of new ones.

Allowing fewer trees with adequate space to grow will result in better and safer trees to be able to grow well and for much longer.

Life in and around trees

Spending time in Savernake forest over three years I was also able to observe the wildlife and plants that live on and grow around the trees. The bark on these ancient giants become very thick and deeply fissured and are perfect for many lichen species that take decades to colonise. Many are so small it needs a hand lens to find them. Others are bushy giving the bark a soft pale green skin. Many small insects include hover flies and gnats that congregate in these fissures and crevices in the bark.

Lesser-stag and red cardinal beetles emerge out of the decaying tree on sunny days to bask on bleached bark while caterpillars graze on fresh green leaves. I found many strange rubbing marks on trunks that could perhaps be made by bats as they forage for insects hiding inside the twisting gnarly bark.

Red admiral butterflies were seen drinking the brown sap oozing from damaged oak bark while being buzzed by hornets. Great and occasionally lesser-spotted woodpecker were heard tapping away on seasoned dead stems as they shimmy to the top most dead branches of maturing stag headed trees.

I caught a glimpse of a lesser-spotted woodpecker on two occasions. A small bird that relies on old trees with decaying branches. This bird is now very rare due to the loss of decaying trees that are rarely left in woodland or on farmland.

My favourite bird, the green woodpecker, was often seen flying over the woodland clearings. Warblers and numerous tits are busy darting in and out of the brambles with the Jenny wren never far away at any time of the year. The occasional grass spider seen scurrying away.

Across the country, health and safety hysteria has been a major cause of the loss of dead and decaying wood from trees, even the smallest dead branches are removed.

The gnarled tree trunks also attract nuthatch and tree creepers and sinister ichneumon wasp exploring every nook and cranny of the ancient oaks.

Exotic coloured vapourer moth caterpillar stand out from the dull hues of shaded boughs below the canopy. Life in the wood is everywhere and is in such contrast from the sterile agrarian landscape just outside the forest.

Deer browsed on bramble and holly retaining in places a more open and diverse woodland understorey.

In the autumn the forest explodes with fungi of all shapes and colours, full of strange chemicals and attached deep down in the soil to a microscopic network of hyphae and mycelium (bootlace like strands) running for hundreds of metres under the forest floor.

New science is showing these organisms, neither a plant nor animal, enable trees to communicate tree to tree, they also enhance the trees survival and possible immune response. So let's not underestimate our trees and the associated flora.

CHAPTER 18

NEW SURROUNDINGS
JUNE 2014

We moved to Herefordshire to a small converted barn just outside Ross-on-Wye. It is set in a rural location with woods nearby but it has taken time getting used to a rather different type of landscape which now surrounds us and the intensive farming practices.

Our dog walks became confined to just a few footpath routes that were kept open while many others had become overgrown or ploughed up. For much of the time we seemed to be wallowing in mud wherever we went.

In January 2016 we lost Bracken at the impressive age for a Labrador of 14, suffering from epilepsy. His system just failed the day after a long walk in the woods. He has left a big hole in our lives and we both miss him greatly.

The last few years I have been working on a project in the

Forest of Dean as part of the Foresters Forest, a lottery bid intended hopefully to revitalise the forest. Over the next few years I am hoping to bring some of my Savernake experience to the Dean and record the remaining ancient and notable trees with volunteers and to raise awareness about the importance of future ancient trees needing open space around them. This will ensure existing and future ancient trees can grow more naturally.

Making a real difference

Coming right up to date I am still working to help safeguard our threatened landscape and wildlife. Although I am still with Plantlife I am now also involved in another new and very ambitious project called "Back from the Brink" I hope everyone hears all about it soon.

Fifty years on it would be a major omission for me not to reflect on where things stand in the countryside as I see it today.

I have genuine concern that there is clear and irrefutable evidence that we are still losing plants and wildlife species.

That every year hectare upon hectare of our once green countryside is being lost by erosion or under buildings and new railway lines.

That our political masters think we can continue with business as usual for years to come.

Today much is being talked about and discussed regarding the environment and the future of Britain, Europe and the planet, so this must be as good a time as any to make some ambitious but vital changes. Action is needed now and I believe we can all do something and we should get on with it. If necessary we can wait for the politicians to catch up but we need to keep them to their word on making our environment better.

How do we do it?

If we are to succeed in restoring our countryside it will require vital change to customs and practices that we have adopted over 50 years in order to reassemble our countryside.

We can only do this by making the right choices and placing real value on nature and natural capital.

We need to rethink nature.

To do this we have to put the vital components back that we have removed through ignorance and to change our presumption that we know better than nature.

- Wildlife and plants cannot choose their destiny, but humans can and to have the type of landscape and environment that respects the natural world.

- We have seen the devastating impact on relying on science to find solutions to constantly fight against nature. Science has to move away from being against nature and to come up with new sustainable solutions and not continue using cocktails of herbicides, pesticides, growth regulators and antibiotics to produce our food.

- We need to allow nature to claim back its space in the woodlands, fields, hedgerows, streams and across the wider countryside. Nature can usually do things better than we can. It is our choice to allow it.

■ We also need to learn to be better at knowing when and how to intervene at the right time and in the right way to ensure biodiversity is enhanced and not degraded or lost.

A machine cannot work without all of its vital components.

The countryside also needs **all** of its vital components to function.

Unlike an expensive machine we do not have to spend lots of money to repair the landscape.

My life can be compared to a tree:

The **roots** are my **experience and acquired wisdom**, a solid base on which my decisions are made.

The **stem** is my strength, **determination** to succeed.

The **canopy** is my passion and **achievements** of a worthwhile and very satisfying life working for nature.

PART 2:

TOMORROW'S CHOICES

CHAPTER 19

OFFERING SOLUTIONS – OUR COUNTRYSIDE TODAY

People often ask me what is wrong with the countryside, it is still green after all!

Since before 1968 right up to 2018 I have continued to watch much of our farmland become less attractive place for nature or seen vital green spaces lost, developed into new building sites. Plants and wildlife continue to decline and placed under serious threat. This is despite all the nature reserves, protected landscapes and enormous efforts being put in by conservation charities and volunteers.

Agriculture and its practices can be divided broadly into two separate and distinct types of farming that is being carried out across Britain.

First are the farms and farmland that local families have

managed for generations practicing traditional farming and who work tirelessly every day on small farmsteads who are still in tune with their environment. Some are passionate and knowledgeable about the wildlife found on their farms. They respect the land and are keen, despite financial difficulties to keep the land in good heart. These are the farms where people can still enjoy nature and deserve support and rewarded for their efforts.

Second are the large agribusiness farms that have intensive operations across thousands of acres of farmland modifying the landscape in favour of optimising crop production. We need to work together to help them find solutions to radically change customs and practices that are damaging the landscape.

Working and walking in the countryside for over 50 years, I have seen with my own eyes a very different landscape both appear and disappear around me and become much poorer to the one I grew up in. It even smells and sounds different today. Much of what was once a rich and diverse countryside has been almost completely lost in some areas. Gone is the colour and with it the wildlife that once lived there which has been displaced to nature reserves and remaining extensively managed farms, or to wild corners in gardens and into the edge-lands of the urban fringe. Our landscape has been transformed.

Much of its original beauty air brushed out.

In our quest for a cheap food and available timber following the two world wars it has really come at a very high price to us all. Our farmers and foresters have done sterling work to produce food and timber as efficiently as they can. Sadly, it also destroyed priceless habitats, birds, insects, flowers and so much more. Over a similar period we have also lost beautiful landscapes without thinking about the cumulative environmental consequences.

The removal of hedgerows and trees, tidying up of decaying wood habitat, the filling in of ponds, draining land and polluting watercourses, the introduction of alien plants and animals and the use of toxic chemicals to control nature. These are all the factors that have conspired (over a very short period in environmental time) to destroy a rich, diverse, and colourful countryside. The cumulative affect has been devastating.

When I moved from a "protected" landscape in the Cotswolds that was sympathetically managed by the National Trust, it was a shock to be reminded of how other parts of the countryside are being so damaged and exploited in order to grow our food in a very different way.

Large characterless fields managed intensively just for agriculture are places where hedges have been removed, few wild flowers grow, where birds or crickets are nowhere to be heard. Many other fields are ploughed right up to low fragmented strips of remnant hedge.

We have over mechanised our landscape. The soil surface changes almost weekly. It is cultivated by increasingly large machinery that is hardly able to fit down the lanes to sow, spray and cut the crops. Harvesting is done at break neck speed and replaced by another crop almost overnight. There is little space or time left for nature to adapt.

Nettles, cleavers, coarse grasses and other nitrogen loving plant bullies have become the dominant beneficiaries of a chemically enriched soil, displacing many other wild plants that once shared the hedge verges but are no longer growing there. The hedges are ruthlessly flailed every year with few, if any, new trees given a chance to develop beyond sapling stage. The lower branches of remaining and all too few older sentinel trees are removed or cut off to make way for machinery. Dead trees and decaying wood removed, frightened by misinterpreted health and safety, misled by thinking that every piece is bound to fall onto someone's head.

Many hedges are now just lines on old maps. Although now protected by law, many of the remaining hedges have become trimmed back to stubs and left unsuitable for nesting song bird or able to offer sanctuary from raptors. No longer offering valuable shelter or food for insects in the search for nectar rich plants.

Field gates are getting wider, some are 30 feet across!

Rural Herefordshire, to mention just one county, grows wheat, barley, potatoes, blueberries, asparagus, rhubarb, beans, strawberries are all grown highly intensively on farms that have become mega businesses. It is frightening to see the extent of soil erosion every time it rains and the amount of chemicals that are cast over plants and food crops every year. The ground is deeply ploughed and becomes compacted. Earthworms and other living organisms are diminished and few nutrients are left. Moles and even wild boar seem to avoid arable fields that have become devoid of their natural food source.

Ted Green[1] is founder member and campaigner for the well-respected Ancient Tree Forum.

Herefordshire is just one of many counties across England being affected by these intensive farming practices.

The legacy of intensive farming and forestry is a dead and degraded soil damaged over a very short space of time. America and Australia have already seen this happen. We should not be standing by and watching it happen here as well.

By raising awareness about this damage that other parts of the world have already suffered from will, I hope, prevent it continuing for much longer in this country.

The *State of Nature Report 2016* confirms that despite all efforts to conserve our nature in the UK, most is still in decline and extinctions are occurring every year. We choose to disregard this at our peril.

In 2018 we need to be even more concerned than ever about how much countryside and open space that we are willing or able to lose under intensive crop production, concrete, tarmac and steel, before nature and our very existence becomes perilous.

Making the right choices tomorrow and over the coming years will become vital to prevent this happening.

Choosing to restore the components in the countryside

Component 1. Increasing trees cover. We are experiencing rising temperatures yet we have fewer trees

---

1. This soil as Ted Green has described, is Toxic!

scattered across the wider landscape too cool the climate than the rest of Europe.

Component 2. Thick and tall hedgerows and in-field trees to provide shade to livestock and assists soil protection. They also lock up carbon, give shelter, perching places and nest sites.

Looking to the future and thinking long term we need more new recruit trees in the right places which are given enough space to grow and reduce the generational gap between the remaining mature trees as they become post mature trees.

Component 3. Retaining dead and decaying wood. We have a serious deficit of large pieces of dead and decaying wood in the countryside because we have chosen to tidy it up, so decaying wood needs to become a vital component again in our countryside.

The English elm trees are living longer in the hedgerows; some are achieving a height up to 25 feet tall, by hugging to the telegraph posts and being missed by the flail. No doubt the utility companies will eventually decide to remove these surviving trees in the future.

Although many believed we had lost all our elm trees forever from disease I am seeing Wych elm returning to the woods and hedgerows again and growing back to a reasonable size, so far, if they are not constantly cut back by flailing. We must avoid the same from happening to the ash trees.

Component 4. Hawthorn and hedgerow trees have been cut down or are severely trimmed annually and a good proportion need to be allowed to grow to full height above the hedges to provide wildlife habitat and produce much needed nectar for insects. It costs nothing to make this choice.

Component 5. Unpolluted ponds and restored waterbodies. These have become scarce in and around fields and woodlands. Many have been filled in or drained and what remain are neglected and losing what is a vital component for wildlife and plants. They can be either temporary or permanent to be valuable.

This is how we can choose to take positive action to restore our landscape with trees and plants and to put the components back into the countryside again.

And we really need to do it sooner than has been suggested in the Government's 25-year Environment Plan.

The wider of benefits of nature in our lives.

1: Why should I choose to care about the countryside?

Agribusiness as well as people living and working in our towns and cities, are no longer seeing nature around them. I think many have become detached from their fundamental and longstanding relationship with the natural world. This detachment has removed any real appreciation for the environment or how it should be treated.

By perpetuating the status quo will further degrade our concern or interest for our environment.

211

Connections with nature for our wellbeing

We know that for the last 50 years the importance and fragility of our natural environment has been greatly underestimated. Our natural environment has been undervalued but over exploited by business, degraded by science and largely overlooked by our education system.

This has resulted in our environment being treated with contempt and as a cash cow. We have a consumer driven, throw away culture, dropping litter, fly tipping our rubbish along roads, in beauty spots, country parks and into the sea.

Fracking is now the next threat we are sleepwalking into

I have even been told "The countryside is a luxury and it can look after itself anyway." I would suggest not.

Not only can a healthy environment produce enormous benefits to every single one of us, it can also save us millions of pounds that is currently being spent on, health, mental health, stress, crime, road repairs, pollution, reducing air quality, flood prevention, and much, much more.

It is time to include this Natural Capital and its benefits into our economic model.

A significant change is needed in the way we all value our countryside, our relationship with it and our reliance upon it.

Long-term visionary thinking and clever investment to restore the environment must be the way forward so it can become a functioning ecosystem that we can all be proud of and which future generations will gain enormous benefit from.

Sustainable ecosystems. Safe and healthy food. Resilience to diseases. A better quality of life. Improved health and wellbeing.

No matter how wealthy we are, we cannot buy any of the above with money.

A new culture of awareness of what is really valuable by informing us better about the food we eat and the products we spend money on could change our attitude towards consumerism and enable us to become more sustainable on our planet. A culture that learns to respects not only nature but also our fellow man.

Our schools and colleges can play an enormously important part in changing our culture and perceptions about the natural world by increasing our knowledge and encouraging us to appreciate our environment better.

One subject, rural science, has been confined to pupils in lower grades and those with learning difficulties or with low expectations of attainment. Environment, farming and horticulture are still considered to be subjects having little, if any, good career prospects or to be of any great use to top stream students!

If we had all been given the opportunity to learn about growing food at school in the 1960s, perhaps organic food production could have become more widely established and much sooner.

In the early eighties, schools phased out domestic science and the opportunity to learn about healthy food and learning cooking skills.

Today we have a serious lack of skills in the woodland, farming and horticultural sector and a declining ability to grow, prepare and cook our food. We need to rely less on apps for ordering take away foods and other necessities and know how to grow and cook healthy food.

2: Choosing to reconnect nature to our human side.

The way we treat our environment reflects the type of people and community that defines us.

Slowly but surely we have gradually and increasingly become detached from our natural roots, relying more on technology for solutions that can damage the environment, such as plastics, chemicals, mining for rare minerals.

I have noticed that people are becoming less confident and uncertain in how they should behave in the natural world or how to treat our environment. We are also becoming obese and try hard to avoid physical work or exercise.

Some people have even become frightened of domestic animals because of their detachment from the natural world around them. Domestic and wild animals are increasingly abused and even tortured.

3: Choosing the natural environment
ahead of technology.

I believe that relying more on IT and smart phones to communicate with and to guide us through everything we do is nothing less than sinister. We are human beings and we are part of nature which means our senses, sight, smell and hearing are all attuned to being used in everyday engagement with fellow human beings and our natural surroundings.

Phones and technology are becoming addictive for some people who are frightened of being out of touch with their device for just a few minutes, just in case they miss a tweet or have to think for themselves! This has resulted in fewer people knowing how to read paper maps or use a compass. Mountain rescues are increasing in number because of people's reliance on using just a mobile phones for navigation. Sat nav systems our unreliable and limits our geographical knowledge to just a narrow line on a map.

I have worked with both urban and rural communities and it is very concerning to see the limited general knowledge that continues to exist about the natural world across all social groups. Paradoxically most people are very interested in the natural world which is borne out by the many millions who watch David Attenborough and other programmes about the environment.

I have found that pretty well everyone I meet is wanting to know more about nature and they are always intrigued when they hear about my own experiences or join me on a

215

walk and spend time around wildlife and trees. By observing people of all ages from many walks of life and hearing what they say and do, I have seen how people change when they re-engage with nature and their environment.

There is however limited access to our natural world already as it is removed from our everyday lives by loss of green spaces and intensive farming and is slowly being replaced more and more by a virtual world for people to experience.

The environment and nature in all its wonder should be a fundamental part of our everyday experience throughout our lives to maintain a connection to the natural world.

I believe that having an insight into our natural world throughout our lives can help to make us healthier and better able to make informed decisions.

I think better contact with the natural world could and should be made available to all our schools through access to trained countryside staff such as rangers who should be resourced to offer a proper professional service.

This can only be successful if well managed natural green spaces were also made available and are accessible nearby. Places where children can sit, play and quietly observe nature, to see flora and fauna on their doorstep.

A more diverse landscape and open spaces could be provided on agricultural land as well as in towns and villages and accessible to all communities which could include, ideally, an arboretum, wild flowers meadows to observe, enjoy and learn about the natural world.

These would be places for people free to socialise and keep

in touch with their community as well as with animals. Places even to camp under the stars and experience a world without technology.

The EU has made the problem worse in some ways by offering subsidies and grants for rigid short term and prescriptive environmental schemes. These have been given mostly to the large agrobusinesses and not to the small farmer or for proper diversification.

Many smaller farms do allow space for nature, so these are the farms that deserve the financial incentives because they are delivering some Natural Capital.

Big business has entered the countryside, often overlooking local empathy and moral responsibility that was once adopted by smaller local landowners stewarding their land for future generations. These large enterprises should be supported but only if they restore the landscape. It will probably save them money in the long run.

Reading the farming press recently the penny may have finally dropped as there does seem to be a welcome move to find solutions to enhance our biodiversity and with stagnation in yields they are keen to improve soil conditions more naturally.

Many farmers voted to leave the EU and are optimistic that there is a better way to manage their land. We all need to work together to achieve this.

4: Choosing to reward the nature professionals

It is nearly 50 years since I left school to follow my chosen profession of managing and conserving the countryside but ignorance and a somewhat low level of importance in this work sadly pervades, even today. Consequently, any paid work in the environmental sector is often thought of as a "nice to have" job. It is usually one of the first jobs to be cut from budgets under pressure. This is happening now across the country.

We know that global warming is a fact and that our environment is being depleted and that we all need a healthy environment in which to live a decent life. We need professional people in the community to do this work.

To conserve our wildlife and manage the environment is complex and challenging.

It has taken decades for me to learn what it is about and I am still learning. Yet despite the increasing level of knowledge and expertise required the sector still attracts a modest or less than average salary compared to other professions. You have only to look at the Countryside Jobs Service web page to see the salaries on offer. It is hardly an attractive career for anyone with or without a degree, wanting a good standard of living, needing to buy a house and raise a family.

Being able to live in the countryside and near to work is pretty well impossible as well.

An average salary today for a qualified Ranger can be between £12,000 and £25,000 per year. They are required to do a challenging job needing a lot initiative, interpersonal skills, be self-motivated, have practical as well as theoretical skills and an understanding of complex processes. As well as a willingness to work all hours and in all weathers. There is no overtime or bonuses

I was paid £18 per week for over a 42-hour week when working as a deer keeper in 1973. I was young then and I learnt a lot from people who knew the work they were doing but it was hardly a fair days pay for very hard and occasionally dangerous work.

Although money is definitely not everything in life and it has never influenced my decision to follow this career, surely as you accumulate experience it should be recognised and fairly rewarded?

I think conservation charities and NGOs have been taken advantage of by governments who heavily rely on them and their volunteers to deliver conservation and environmental protection without paying for it. The dedication and vision by these people and organisations have seen the successful re reintroduced of the red kite, brought back the bittern and large blue butterfly from extinction in England and hopefully will restore more of our species and habitats in coming years.

These people are actually maintaining all of our quality of life and we all rely on their wisdom and devotion. Many are well qualified staff, others are keen volunteers who surely deserve better reward and support?

So why do we not reward them fairly and in proportion to what we seem happy to reward a footballer or a banker?

The limited resources provided by the state in the UK for our environment continue to reduce each year and it becomes harder to find alternative funding. Yet other countries less wealthy than ours do invest a lot more in their environment.

Although I have already explained that I was not academic or a fast track learner and was useless at sport, I have nevertheless continued to be a self-developer and have taught myself a wide range of subjects and skills. This has been done by gaining practical, first-hand experience over many years.

A similar approach but better structured should be available for people keen to enter their chosen profession. Apprenticeships in environmental management has to be an option that should be made more available.

Through my own efforts and determination it has resulted in me being fully employed most of the time since leaving school in 1971. However, it should not have been as difficult to achieve as it actually was. There are many good people who have not been so lucky or successful and have been lost from this very worthwhile profession.

More choices.

5. Choosing to allow our trees to grow old.

An ancient tree develops a low and wide crown of branches as the trunk of the tree becomes fatter and hollows with age. The lower centre of gravity also gives the tree more stability against high winds. Our oldest trees need greater protection and long term management to live longer, become more biodiverse and to enhance our landscape. They are irreplaceable and should be non-negotiable.

6. Choosing to protect the soil.

With increasing risk of flooding often caused by inappropriate land management it is widely acknowledged that trees and shrubs can become part of the armoury needed to reduce flood damage and soil erosion. They can also enhance soil fertility so future policies are forward thinking to plan much further ahead.

- Water run-off is a serious problem today, much of it is coming off farmland fields and flooding roads and communities. Perhaps the changes we have made to that farmland is the reason?
- Integrating farming more with woodland management and include agroforestry as part of future farm enterprises, where it can fit well into the landscape.

A new and positive development is that Agroecology is a subject now being discussed more and available to students at Harper Adams Agriculture College which links more closely the benefits of farming with the environment.

- Using our land differently and in more than one dimension to use the space above the ground in multiple tiers, offers enormous potential of producing more from the same surface area.

Appendix I.

Ways to rebuild the landscape in LESS than 25 years.
Land Management best practices. A checklist.

- by not cultivating field margins, allowing a minimum of two to three metres wide buffer strips either side along the base of hedges and along watercourses.

- leaving field corners and land with poor fertility to regenerate naturally and allow 20% dead and decaying native wood to become a feature around the farm margins; avoid chipping and the removal of all dead wood fallen or standing.

- Reduce ploughing and increase direct drilling.

- Establishing grass leys to include herbage.

- Reduce use of antibiotics.

- Reduce chemical fertiliser input.

- Leaving hedges to grow broader, thicker and taller by less frequent cutting.

- Reduce the use of flail, lay some sections of hedge over a seven to ten year frequency.

- Remove the build-up of cut material and enriched soil nutrients from hedge bottoms.

- Re-open and maintain old ditches and ponds.

- Create ponds and wetlands on farms where ground conditions allow and where there is historical precedent.

- Protect all water courses from chemical spray run off and any silt entering the water.

- Establish open water in woods for some of the year at least.

- Use local traditional livestock breeds more.

- Graze woodland with cattle while also reducing overall cattle and sheep numbers on the farm.

- Leave fields fallow for three months to allow worm/bacteria infestation to decrease.

- Work together with neighbouring farms and landowners to manage grey squirrel, and deer if their impact is high.

- Manage some newly planted woodlands as coppice for wood fuel.

- Establish woodland meadows with standard trees as part of good woodland, farm environmental management.

- Promote establishment of wild flowers and areas of scrub.

- Allow standard native trees of differing ages to regenerate in hedgerows. Give them adequate space.

- Retain large amounts of decaying and dead wood fallen and standing, within woodland, hedges and in field corners. Be content to be less tidy.

- Restore existing orchards and plant new orchards, retain old trees.

- Encourage natural regeneration of native trees in fields and fruit trees in hedgerows.

- Offer new and alternative routes across farmland for public enjoyment and to separate people (dogs)from livestock.

- Protect livestock in buildings from wild animals entering.

Measuring Success? We can measure success by seeing the following put into practice:

- Potential recruit ancient trees are being left to grow in the hedges and in woodland to replace old and diseased trees? Potential ancient trees of the future are being given adequate space to grow that will enable them to live beyond 500 years?

- Some hedges grow thick and have flower rich margins that are not flailed or ploughed up annually.

- The soil is managed to maintain and increase its organic content. Measures to prevent it becoming increasingly degraded through intensive practices are in place in the short to medium term.

- Less ploughing and more direct drilling is being done.

- Growers find alternatives to the use of neonicotinoids and consider our native bees and many other insects as being beneficial to growing of crops.

- Bees are not needed to be imported in boxes onto farms to pollinate fruit trees.

- Naturally occurring nectar producing wild plants are encouraged to grow along the field margins and are not cut until late summer early autumn.

- The use of chemicals including antibiotics is reduced and more genetically resilient plants and livestock are used.

- New recreational/environment parks are established where new development is placing unsustainable pressures on existing open spaces and protected areas. Their role to provide focussed landscape enhancement measures outside of existing protected areas by giving positive support to landowners, parish councils and support organisations. This can begin to achieve a joined-up landscape able to function again ecologically.

- Integrated training courses are available in colleges and work placements to train land managers including farmers, foresters, land owners, rangers and wardens. The tutors to include practitioners and representatives from the conservation organisations including; communication skills, ecology, agriculture, woodland management, botany, zoology, animal husbandry, hydrology, land history and even practical problem solving. (Life skills).

- national apprenticeship scheme established to develop a new Wildlife Management Network of practical advisers, across all habitats, to inform and guide best practice on integrated land use.

- People resources are used to maintain the environment by using schools, colleges, offenders and prisoners as part of their education and rehabilitation to implement environmental management work. This could include low skill activities such as litter and fly tipping clearance. Using all sectors of the community to become aware of and to take it seriously and reduce it happening.

The cost benefits of this approach in managing green capital assets will offer opportunities for different professions to work closer together to manage ecosystems and wildlife populations and to gain a better understanding of the natural resource.

Halt the loss of Ecological Capital that is being lost at great cost to our population and threatens our quality of life.

Funding for environmental management and enhancement including acquisition of land to come from public departments who are currently squandering millions of pounds on repairs and damage limitation caused by neglect of the environment.

To move away from short term, stop and start, grants and policies. Nature cannot and does not work this way.

Development rights and changes in Planning.

This book began with a reference to my Town Planning grandfather so it would seem appropriate to include suggestions here to summarise the changes based on my own experience of the current planning process that are still needed to ensure our communities are able to enjoy a good quality of life and our rich countryside is not lost forever.

Building and development is currently out of control, seriously affecting the landscape and degrading vital green capital. This is continuing to put wildlife and biodiversity at risk. The planning departments need radical reform to place a greater strategic emphasis in association with a new Environment Department for the protection, restoration, and maintenance of green spaces before, during and after all new development.

1. Condition on all new development to ensure a proportion of new homes are truly affordable and for the development to be sustainable with the inclusion of adequate green space being provided as part of any new scheme. To also mitigate environmental loss and damage and to prevent pressure increasing on existing open spaces including protected landscapes, NNRs and SACs.

2. New special designation for some farmland in national parks to diversify land for open space recreation to protect natural capital for public benefit.

3. For farmland to be able to diversify to become parks, arboretum and sanctuaries for nature.

4   Roadside verges managed sympathetically together with adjacent farmland for flowers, trees and shrubs that are encouraged by natural regeneration. Reduce mass planting of trees and shrubs to allow more diversity with fewer plants to grow naturally. Quality rather than quantity.

5. Old railway lines recommissioned and reconnected to offer better access to towns and nearby villages for pedestrians and cyclists. These corridors are also valuable for wildlife.

6. New roads and railway line construction to include tunnels built under protected or environmentally sensitive areas and or overhead crossing points (green bridges) for wildlife are installed to maintain landscape connectivity.

7   Identifying most suitable locations for solar farm sites in advance will provide opportunities for planning on a landscape scale for habitat connectivity and enhancements. Solar and green energy producers can become part of the solution to increase natural forage areas for wildlife away from more intensively farmed land and help reconnect landscapes. Design and management agreements for these facilities need to be conditional before allowing any development.

Appendix II. Post Brexit.

A STRATEGY for a Country Fit to Manage its Environment.

There is a fundamental duty placed on Government to manage sustainably a joined up landscape for our food, water, timber and for people.

This requires a ground-up remodelling of the Environment department to make it fit for purpose post Brexit, better able to deliver its Environment Plan and make the changes that are needed.

Following the recent political change of direction in the UK and the USA it is becoming increasingly important to make positive changes in favour of the environment and this is a golden opportunity to use our new independence to create a sustainable and resilient model for our countryside, the urban fringes, the inner cities and for all the people who live in these places.

Below I have proposed an alternative structure to how I think we could manage our environment much better and be better able to deliver an Environment Plan.

Alternative structure for Defra to become Department of Environment Agriculture Natural Resource - DEANaR

Step 1. (An Organogram)

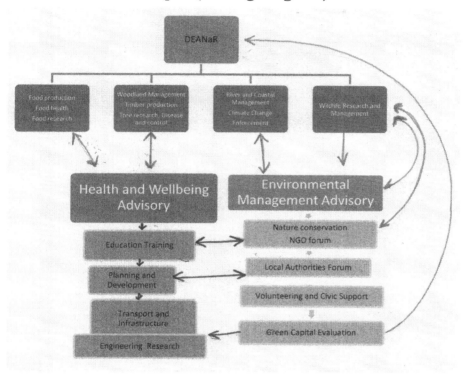

Establish a new Department for Environment, Agriculture and Natural Resource. (DEANR) to be set up and devoted to biodiversity, to be responsible for and oversee the following:

Wildlife and countryside management including woodland creation and management, sustainable food and timber production and management practices, protection of soils, river and water quality, research into plant diseases, the impact of climate change.

All the above to have links to recreation, education, planning and health departments. Supermarkets and the food regulation industry.

Linking and integrating these activities will ensure they become better connected and understood and that measures are in place to both protect and enhance landscape, while also produce safe sustainable food, timber and minerals.

A forum of external NGO organisations and other agencies could help to advise the new Natural Resource Department and help design new well informed policies.

These organisations to be contracted to carry out conservation work on private land and to support the agriculture sector. This will need funding to do this but they must stay politically independent.

Demonstration farms and woodland that are implementing management to show best sustainable practices. These set up across the country to include a wide range of landscapes and habitats. To explore opportunities for pop up Knepp Estates to be established to restore badly degraded ecosystems.

Extend and enlarge existing public parks where adjacent land is available using agricultural land that is fragmented, degraded or is unviable.

Paul Brueton Rutter

January 2018

A CAUTIONARY TALE

If we continue as we are and do not change anything the following true account of a country walk will I fear become typical.

2017 Herefordshire Country Walk.

I have just returned from a walk near my home. This is a part of England revered for its rural landscape and rich countryside of oaks, apple orchards and cider, so you may be surprised to read that the countryside is dying and slowly disappearing.

It was a glorious warm July summer evening, bathed in golden sunlight, so I decided to enjoy a country stroll something I have always done since my childhood. I start my walk in a large field with rows of fruit bushes. The farm track at the entrance to the field is a fine, red material resembling a sandy beach, the result of constant traffic by tractors and other farm vehicles.

There were also small areas fenced off with string along the hedge displaying small posters saying; Rest Area and then a few yards away Smoking Area! A portable plastic toilet sentry box was located a few yards further away. A requirement it seems under health and safety for the fruit pickers.

At the bottom end of the field was stagnant standing water, this was residual run off from the field and the water was thick with green algae. It was seeping through the hedge onto the adjacent road.

Between the ranks of fruit bushes the grass had been mowed regularly and the surrounding field margin had also just been strimmed down to just a few centimetres. This was in early July, on the hottest day of the year. Quite apart from the noise made by the strimmers for two days, I did feel sorry for the guys doing this hot dusty and seemingly unnecessary work and wondered what was gained by cutting the margins of wild plants around the field.

The rows of fruit bushes had polystyrene boxes mounted on stands 200 yards apart or so. These contained colonies of imported bees perched on pallets in full sunlight and used to just pollinate the fruit bushes.

I continued my walk along the dry path around the edge of the field, I see some pigeons and crows and can hear the bird alarms hidden in the fruit bushes making electronic squawking sounds.

This field has a public footpath but although local people had confirmed in the neighbourhood plan, of their need to enjoy the countryside, footpaths are overgrown, the stiles and way markers are missing or are covered by bramble and nettles. I pondered why the resident strimming team did not cut it from this stile?

I had to push my way through a gap in the undergrowth to use a field gate to reach the lane, taking me towards the nearby hamlet. The lane is an ancient winding route established centuries ago by horses and wagons and worn into high banks with hedges of hawthorn, hazel and even a few small elm trees.

This country lane is now regularly used by the largest HGV lorries taking produce to supermarkets and to Europe, so the hedges are flailed harshly throughout the year.

One elm tree grows strongly above the hedge; it is clinging against a telegraph pole so has been the fortunate one, spared from destruction by the frequent hedge flailing. The elm was once the most common roadside tree before Dutch Elm arrived in the seventies. Sadly in haste we cut them all down and have continued to cut hedges very low that has prevented the return of these and other statuesque trees to our hedgerows. The ash tree may well be the next casualty leaving us with even fewer trees.

A little further along the lane I pass a fine ancient oak tree with its broad spreading crown probably well over 300 years old, a witness to so much change that has occurred around it. The oak tree now stands precariously next to the road and is being passed on one side by the enormous juggernauts; while in autumn tractors with ploughs cut into the turf frighteningly close to the base of the tree on the other side of the hedge. The tree is hollowing and maturing slowly so I really hope it can survive and continue to be one of the remaining old features left. No young oaks are growing in any of the surrounding hedges.

I am passed, just inches away, by a car travelling at speed, oblivious it seems to my presence.

While this is a "quiet" country lane it has no grass verge anymore so is very hazardous to pedestrians and dog walkers being the only route available out of the village. I am pleased therefore to leave the lane and return again to green grass beneath my feet. The small paddock I cross is one of few now that have grass growing and is grazed by sheep this year but the next field that was also grazed last year is over a metre tall in a rape seed crop. The footpath here although waymarked on the gatepost soon disappears into long grass, thistles and into the rape.

I push my way again through the vegetation and up to a large badger sett that was active the last time I walked this route about two months ago. These setts are protected by law but the plough has cultivated the ground right up to the entrances, which are immersed in the rape and are inactive, no signs of life, no footprints.

I continue my walk along the footpath, now a narrow strip of unploughed ground between the field and a heavily silted stream; potatoes are growing in this and the other surrounding fields. I am sprayed by cascading water sent high into the air by an irrigator pumping water out of the brook and over the trees, much of it not actually reaching the crop.

The field opens out here to a distant view over the low cut hedges up to the nearby ancient woodland where a traditional stone barn sits perfectly under the canopy of a line of ancient oak trees. They have survived felling and the modern forestry planting close behind them but are being affected by heavy shade from alien conifers growing fast towards them.

The rest of my walk is devoid of any other wildlife; no birds, insects or wildflowers to be seen, even on such a perfect evening, only rank grass and nettles. The brook has been widened to accommodate pipes for the irrigating pumps and the next field I enter has more bare soil. The noise and smell of a large diesel engine of another irrigator fills the valley now, echoing against the nearby woodland, then a rabbit runs for cover as I pass more potatoes being grown on raised ridges of more dry, thirsty soil.

Deep eroded channels run across this bare soil taking the fertility down to the stream, and is reminder of recent heavy rainfall.

Approaching the lane again the field opposite is covered by ranks of curving plastic structures.

These are polytunnels and are used to force the growth of fruit to reach the shops early in the season. Many hectares of these plastic tunnels are increasingly covering the county including in the Areas of Outstanding Natural Beauty.

As I leave the farmland I see a pair of mute swans proudly swimming with their two cygnets on a water storage pond and I think how incongruous they look learning to swim gracefully in this sterile reservoir surrounded by a landscape covered in plastic and I wonder what the cygnets think of this new countryside in 2017?

Alas they did not survive.